T0323929

DIET AND FIGHTING BLADDER CANCER

DIET AND FIGHTING BLADDER CANCER

DR. MAURICE ZEEGERS

ELSEVIER

ACADEMIC PRESS
An imprint of Elsevier

Academic Press is an imprint of Elsevier
125 London Wall, London EC2Y 5AS, United Kingdom
525 B Street, Suite 1650, San Diego, CA 92101, United States
50 Hampshire Street, 5th Floor, Cambridge, MA 02139, United States
The Boulevard, Langford Lane, Kidlington, Oxford OX5 1GB, United Kingdom

Notices
Knowledge and best practice in this field are constantly changing. As new research and
experience broaden our understanding, changes in research methods, professional
practices, or medical treatment may become necessary.

Practitioners and researchers must always rely on their own experience and knowledge in
evaluating and using any information, methods, compounds, or experiments described
herein. In using such information or methods they should be mindful of their own safety
and the safety of others, including parties for whom they have a professional
responsibility.

To the fullest extent of the law, neither the Publisher nor the authors, contributors, or
editors, assume any liability for any injury and/or damage to persons or property as a
matter of products liability, negligence or otherwise, or from any use or operation of any
methods, products, instructions, or ideas contained in the material herein.

Library of Congress Cataloging-in-Publication Data
A catalog record for this book is available from the Library of Congress

British Library Cataloguing-in-Publication Data
A catalogue record for this book is available from the British Library

ISBN: 978-0-12-814677-4

For information on all Academic Press publications visit our website at
https://www.elsevier.com/books-and-journals

Publisher: Stacy Masucci
Acquisition Editor: Rafael Teixeira
Editorial Project Manager: Megan Ashdown
Production Project Manager: Debasish Ghosh
Cover Designer: Mark Rogers

Typeset by TNQ Technologies

Working together
to grow libraries in
developing countries

www.elsevier.com • www.bookaid.org

Contents

Contributors

Maree Brinkman
Department of Clinical Studies and Nutritional Epidemiology, Nutrition Biomed Research Institute, Carlton, Victoria, Australia

Marian de van der Schueren
HAN University of Applied Sciences, Nijmegen, The Netherlands

Marieke van den Beuken-van Everdingen
Centre of Expertise for Palliative Care, Maastricht University Medical Centre (MUMC+), Maastricht, The Netherlands

Frits van Osch
VieCurie Medical Centre, Venray, The Netherlands

Marga van Slooten
Cook & Care, Haarlem, The Netherlands

Anke Wesselius
NUTRIM School for Nutrition and Translational Research in Metabolism, Maastricht University, Maastricht, The Netherlands

Maurice Zeegers
Care and Public Health Research Institute, Maastricht University, Maastricht, The Netherlands

Introduction

Foreword

With so much information coming from all directions, on different diets, foods, nutrients, and supplements on what to have once you have been diagnosed with bladder cancer, it can be overwhelming for the cancer patient and their families/carers. While most of this dietary advice is well meaning, it is usually conflicting and quite often controversial and unfortunately not evidence based. This book provides bladder cancer patients and the layman with an excellent guide on what is currently the best available dietary guidelines for all stages of the bladder cancer journey. This is a great resource to empower patients and to use in conjunction with their medical team's advice.

Dr. Maree Brinkman

Accredited Practising Dietitian & Nutritional Oncology Research
Nutrition Biomed Research Institute, Melbourne, Australia

About the author

Dr. Maurice Zeegers has dedicated his career to researching bladder cancer, during which he has directed numerous research studies and randomized clinical trials to investigate the relationship between nutrition and urinary bladder carcinogenesis. He has published over 250 peer-reviewed scientific papers in the highest-ranked academic journals and is regularly invited to speak on the topic at international scientific conferences. Dr. Zeegers currently holds a Chair in Complex Genetics and Epidemiology as full professor at Maastricht University in the Netherlands, where he also serves as its Head of School and as Director of CAPHRI, the Care and Public Health Research Institute. He acts as the vice president of the European Epidemiology Federation and holds honorary professorships in England, Belgium, and China.

From the author

Every year, half a million of people worldwide are diagnosed with urinary bladder cancer. Although many patients wonder what they can do to influence this disease, mainly via their diet, a book about the relationship between diet and bladder cancer had not been written. The existing information on the internet is varied, sometimes contradictory, sometimes overinterpreted, and sometimes even wrong. I have devoted my career to researching bladder cancer becoming somewhat of a specialist in this field. It is my duty to share with you what I learned. The book gives an honest reflection on what scientists currently know, but also what they don't yet know about how diet contributes to all stages of this important disease, from prevention to treatment to palliative care.

This book has not been possible without the input of my colleagues, both clinicians and scientists. Here I would like to mention Frits van Osch, Sylvia Jochems, Anke Wesselius, Maree Brinkman, Marieke van den Beuken-van Everdingen, and Marian de van der Schueren. Please see the footnote[1] for a list of the coauthors for each chapter.

We endeavored to use a no-nonsense approach with rich and up-to-date references to the academic scientific literature on the relevant topic. The primary audience is bladder cancer patients who wish to be well-informed, although clinicians and scientists may also find the book an interesting read and may wish to use the academic references to dig a little deeper. Over 100 references to the academic literature can be found in Appendix 1. These references form the backbone of this book. As the science on diet and bladder cancer is evolving quickly, I promise to update this book every five years.

Although the content of the book is purely science-based, we tried to write the book in an easy-to-read format, illustrated with tasty recipes. This forms the other backbone of this book. Marga van Slooten a chef from www.CookandCare.nl, who specializes in cooking for cancer patients, took on the challenge of translating the scientific findings into practical and example recipes. Marga cooked all recipes twice, and Stefanie Spoelder made beautiful photographs to illustrate this. The recipes are found close to where the relationship between the recipe and the findings is discussed, but you will see that many recipes also suit other places. If you want to know exactly which recipe relates to which recommendation, please have a look at Appendix 2.

I wish you all the best in your journey to fight bladder cancer.

Dr. Maurice P.A. Zeegers
Professor of Complex Genetics and Epidemiology
m.zeegers@fightingcancerwithfood.org

---

[1]Chapter 1: Frits van Osch, Maurice Zeegers
Chapter 2: Anke Wesselius, Marga van Slooten, Maurice Zeegers
Chapter 3: Marga van Slooten, Maurice Zeegers
Chapter 4: Anke Wesselius, Marga van Slooten, Maurice Zeegers
Chapter 5: Maree Brinkman, Marga van Slooten, Maurice Zeegers
Chapter 6: Marieke van den Beuken-van Everdingen, Marian de van der Schueren, Maurice Zeegers
Appendix 1: Maurice Zeegers
Appendix 2: Marga van Slooten

CHAPTER 1

Who gets bladder cancer?

Frits van Osch[1], Maurice Zeegers[2]
[1]VieCurie Medical Centre, Venray, The Netherlands; [2]Care and Public Health Research Institute, Maastricht University, Maastricht, The Netherlands

Contents

Bladder cancer is the ninth most common cancer worldwide, and it is more prevalent in Western countries.[1] Even though bladder cancer is relatively common, the number of patients who die from it is relatively low. This is possibly because the bladder is surgically removed when the disease presents itself in a more advanced stage. Also, bladder cancer is often diagnosed early so it can be treated effectively.[2] Nevertheless, bladder cancer is known for its high risk of recurrence, which has a large impact on quality of life and generates high disease management costs from a public health perspective. Bladder cancer is thus a disease that we would like to eliminate—first, by doing everything to prevent it in the first place, and second, once bladder cancer is there, to reduce its impact on the lives of patients. In this chapter, we will explain what is known about why people get bladder cancer and what you can do to fight it. In contrast to the other chapters in this book, this chapter does not focus on the dietary aspects of bladder cancer.

Diet and Fighting Bladder Cancer
ISBN 978-0-12-814677-4
https://doi.org/10.1016/B978-0-12-814677-4.00001-0
1

1.1 How do you get bladder cancer and how is it treated?

Bladder cancer is most often diagnosed after finding blood in your urine. Other important symptoms include noticeable changes in urinary frequency and urgency, as well as a burning sensation when urinating.[3] Sometimes, a urologist will find blood in your urine because of bladder inflammation. However, if bladder cancer is detected it can be broadly divided into two categories: non-muscle-invasive bladder cancer (NMIBC), previously also called superficial bladder cancer, and muscle-invasive bladder cancer (MIBC).[4,5] These two categories are biologically different and are therefore also treated differently. The difference between these two types of bladder cancer are shown in Fig. 1.1. Approximately 70%−80% of bladder cancers are non-muscle-invasive when discovered at diagnosis.[1,6] NMIBC has a better chance of survival than MIBC, however bladder cancer in NMIBC patients is known to frequently recur within a few years.[6]

There are different explanations for why you could get bladder cancer. Most scientists agree that several compounds that must be removed from the body through urine are able to cause cancer by interacting with the bladder wall. An important

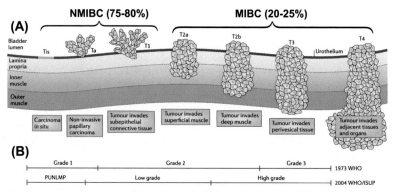

Figure 1.1 Schematic depiction of different stages of bladder cancer, showing the differences between non-muscle-invasive bladder cancer (NMIBC) and muscle-invasive bladder cancer (MIBC).[7]

characteristic of all potentially carcinogenic compounds is that they can damage the bladder wall repeatedly whenever there is urine in the bladder. Being exposed to damage from carcinogenic compounds over a long period of time can result in changes to the behavior of cells and ultimately in the formation of cancer cells in the bladder wall.

NMIBCs are generally treated by removing the tumor using a cystoscope (also called a resectoscope), followed by long-term monitoring and several check-ups. Chemotherapy is commonly used as an additional treatment and mostly consists of Bacillus Calmette-Guerin recommended for high-risk patients (patients with larger tumors, for example) or Mitomycin C intermediate-risk patients.[2,4] When tumors invade the muscular layer, or go beyond that, they are called muscle-invasive. Standard treatment for MIBC is chemotherapy followed by removal of the bladder, also called radical cystectomy.[2,5] However, as removing the bladder is a major surgical procedure with many possible side effects, studies into alternative therapy options have been performed. For example, it has been shown that a combination of chemotherapy and radiotherapy without removal of the bladder can achieve long-term positive outcomes comparable to those of chemotherapy and surgical removal.[8]

1.2 Where does bladder cancer occur and why does it differ between countries?

Bladder cancer is most commonly diagnosed in men. Nevertheless, over the past 10 years, the gender gap is narrowing. This is most likely explained by the decreasing number of male smokers compared to female smokers worldwide, as smoking is the major risk factor for bladder cancer.[9] It is, however, very likely that there are other factors than smoking alone that contribute to an increased risk of bladder cancer. When looking at the global statistics, the gap in number of diagnoses between males and females is very clear (see Fig. 1.2). Scientists use the word "incidence" to describe the number of new cases

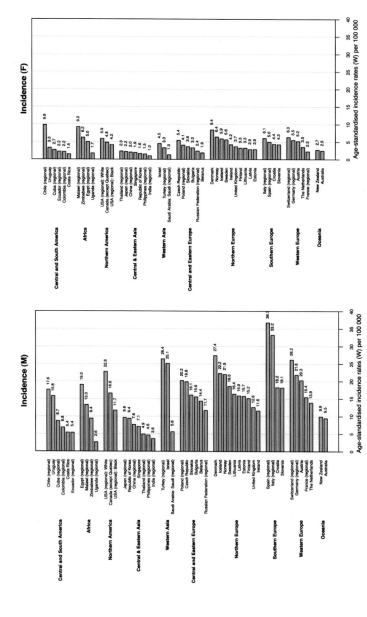

Figure 1.2 Age-standardized incidence rates of bladder cancer in men (left) and women (right) in selected countries from 2003 to 2007 (Egypt: 2004–2007).[1]

(frequency) that are diagnosed over a certain period (for example, a year).

Fig. 1.2 also reveals that Europe and North America as well as Western Asia have the highest incidence rates of bladder cancer diagnoses between 2003 and 2007, while the incidence rate is much lower in Central and Eastern Asia, South America, and Oceania. Similar trends were also observed before 2004. This has led many scientists to believe that the Western diet and other health-related behaviors that are more prevalent in Westernized countries might be associated with the formation of bladder cancer (see Chapter 4). Fortunately, the number of people diagnosed with bladder cancer is slowly decreasing in most countries. This trend is reminiscent of the decreasing number of smokers in most of these countries over the past 20-odd years.[1] Because cancer does not form overnight, we are required to look at patterns of risk behavior that happened many years before diagnosis to know why bladder cancer occurs in a population.

Bladder cancer is a type of cancer that is most commonly diagnosed in the elderly. For example, in the United Kingdom about 70% of cases are diagnosed in patients aged 70 years or older.[10] As there is a larger proportion of elderly people globally, there is a larger burden of bladder cancer in countries with a high life expectancy rate, as reflected in global statistics. Fortunately, if you were diagnosed today, it is more likely that you would have smaller tumors that can be treated more efficiently than 20 years ago. In the past, the disease would probably have been diagnosed at a later stage, when you would need high-impact treatment. At this later stage, the disease could easily have resulted in death. Nowadays, a lot of research into noninvasive screening methods for bladder cancer, such as urine tests that can detect remnants of bladder cancer cells in urine and detect bladder cancer much earlier, is occurring.[11] Considering all these factors we now see that the incidence of bladder cancer is indeed higher in an aging population, but with many patients who are diagnosed in an early stage of disease, when the cancer was able to be treated more effectively.

1.3 Risk factors for bladder cancer and the impact on public health and individuals

The best-identified risk factors for bladder cancer are smoking[12] and occupational exposure to carcinogenic chemicals (e.g., in rubber workers or hair dressers).[13] Smoking has been studied extensively in the past decades, and it has been shown that the total number of years smoking is the most important factor in determining bladder cancer, because if you smoke longer, you are most exposed to the potentially harmful effects of cigarette smoke in the urine.[14] Being a (lifelong) smoker at the time of diagnosis of bladder cancer could even increase your risk of the bladder cancer recurring.[15] Therefore completely abstaining from or quitting smoking if you already smoke is recommended at any age for any person in order to significantly decrease the risk of bladder cancer. While smoking explains 40–50% of bladder cancer cases,[12] there are still many other possible risk factors that explain why people who do not smoke also get bladder cancer.

1.4 Conclusion and rationale for this book

Having said this, apart from stopping smoking, increasing physical activity[16] and not drinking water polluted by arsenic,[17] no other lifestyle modifications have been established so far that irrefutably lower the risk of bladder cancer. Since studying how diet is involved in preventing or causing diseases is very complex, neither single food items nor dietary patterns have been established as major modifiable risk factors for bladder cancer yet. However, there are several promising leads concerning diet, which will be explored in this book, based on studies on bladder cancer as well as other types of cancer. For now, the best we can do is explain these leads and make general recommendations regarding food elements, until more scientific evidence concerning diet and bladder cancer comes to light.

CHAPTER 2

Can fluid intake help to prevent bladder cancer?

Anke Wesselius[1], Marga van Slooten[2], Maurice Zeegers[3]

[1]NUTRIM School for Nutrition and Translational Research in Metabolism, Maastricht University, Maastricht, The Netherlands; [2]Cook & Care, Haarlem, The Netherlands; [3]Care and Public Health Research Institute, Maastricht University, Maastricht, The Netherlands

Contents

Although some water is obtained through foods, most fluids are consumed through drinking water and other beverages. Over the years, various recommendations on daily fluid intake have been made, including the recommendation to consume six to eight glasses of fluids per day.[18] However, the actual amount of fluid that each individual needs per day can vary depending on sex, age, weight, physical activity level, medication use, and the humidity level of the air on that specific day.[19] But how can drinking fluids help you fight bladder cancer? In this chapter, we will explain what is known about fluid intake and the risk of developing bladder cancer and what you can do to lower your chances of getting this disease. This is also the first chapter in which we give you example recipes based on the knowledge we have today.

Diet and Fighting Bladder Cancer
ISBN 978-0-12-814677-4
https://doi.org/10.1016/B978-0-12-814677-4.00002-2

2.1 The urinary tract

After your kidneys filter waste from your blood and produce urine, the urine is transported to your bladder via thin tubes called ureters. The urine is then stored in your bladder until it is emptied through the urethra (Fig. 2.1).

Besides water, salts, ammonia, urochrome (which gives the yellow color), and waste products (urea and creatinine), urine can contain carcinogens, for example from cigarette smoke, which come into contact with the wall of the bladder until urination. In general, the more fluids you drink, the faster you'll empty your bladder, therefore the less time your bladder wall is exposed to these carcinogens. This literally means that one way to reduce your risk of bladder cancer is to reduce the time your bladder comes into contact with these carcinogens,[20–23] although this is strictly not a dietary recommendation. In other words, **empty your bladder regularly by urinating frequently.**

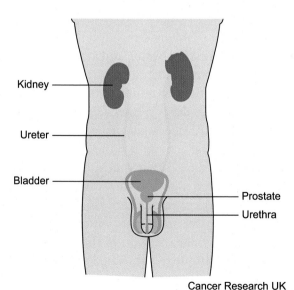

Cancer Research UK

Figure 2.1 Urinary tract. *(Adapted from www.cancerresearchuk.org.)*

2.2 Fluid intake

The first landmark paper that suggested a possible relationship between fluid intake and bladder was based on a 1999 U.S. study of almost 50,000 male health professionals, one of the largest studies of its kind at that time. The researchers found that high daily fluid intake appeared to lower the risk of bladder cancer.[24] However, after 12 additional years of research studies, there appeared to be a relationship between drinking more fluids in general and bladder cancer risk,[25] without taking into account the type of fluids that are consumed. Smokers have a higher risk of bladder cancer (see Chapter 1); a study in 2012 indicated that by drinking more water, the capacity of the urine to cause DNA damage was indeed lower.[26] This observation was confirmed by two later studies among female nurses, suggesting that drinking more fluids may lower bladder cancer risk in smokers.[25] However, most studies carried out up to today have found no clear relationship between drinking more fluids in general and lowering the risk of bladder cancer.[9,27–47] It has even been hypothesized that drinking more fluids may actually increase bladder cancer risk, as carcinogens in urine can also reach deeper into layers of the bladder wall when the bladder stretches to hold more fluid if you don't empty your bladder regularly.[48–50] For this reason, the debate among scientists whether high fluid intake is healthy or not is still ongoing. A possible explanation is that it is not fluid intake as such but your urination habits that count, which is of course related, as was outlined in the previous paragraph. Another likely explanation is that different types of beverages may play a different role in bladder cancer, and it is more important than just look at the total amount of fluid you drink per day.

Fruity water (drinks)

It is important to drink plenty of water every day. Fruit-infused water can be an attractive and healthy option.

It is not hard to make, and you can create all sorts of flavors. Use organic products where possible. This is especially important if you use the skin of a fruit or vegetable.

Recipe
What you need and how to prepare it.
Ingredients
- 4 cups of water (we recommend using filtered or mineral water, but you can also use tap water if the quality is good)
- Ice cubes (optional)
- Pieces of fresh fruit or vegetables. Possible combinations:
  - $1/4$ cucumber thinly sliced, 1 lime in pieces, a few mint leaves
  - 2 slices of lemon, 4 slices of cucumber, 1 piece of ginger
  - 1 piece of watermelon, mashed with the hand blender; $1/2$ lemon or orange, pressed
  - $1/2$ green apple cut in thin pieces, a handful of raspberries, and 1 sprig of rosemary or mint
  - 1 orange cut in small pieces, 1 cinnamon stick, 1 inch of ginger cut into thin slices
  - $1/2$ lemon cut in thin pieces, a handful of raspberries

Preparation
Put the fruit or vegetables of your choice in a large pitcher. If necessary, bruise the ingredients with a fork to release more juices.

Add any herbs shortly before serving; otherwise, the taste may be too strong. Fill the pitcher with water and ice cubes. Keep the fruit-infused water in the refrigerator until use (Fig. 2.2).

Figure 2.2 Fruity water.

2.3 Arsenic and chlorine in drinking water

Research into fluid intake and bladder cancer has been complicated by drinking water containing arsenic.[51,52] Research has shown that exposure to more than 10 µg/L of arsenic in drinking water may increase the risk of bladder cancer,[51] and therefore the World Health Organization and the US Food and Drug Administration decided in 2006 that arsenic concentrations in drinking water must never exceed this concentration.[53] While concentrations of arsenic in drinking water are now low in North America and almost nonexistent in Europe, in parts of Southeast Asia and South America levels are still significantly higher,[54] potentially causing bladder cancer. So, if you live in Southeast Asia or South America, you may want to **ask your government about the current arsenic concentrations in your drinking water**. Another chemical found in water is chlorine. When added to water chlorine breaks down into trihalomethanes, which eliminate harmful bacteria (36). When combined with filtration, adding chlorine is an excellent way to disinfect water. This is the reason why it is used in swimming pools and drinking supplies. Long-term consumption of chlorinated drinking water, however, seems to be associated with bladder cancer, particularly in men. Nevertheless, according to a metastudy of other research studies, chlorine is likely to be a small player in the fight against bladder cancer.[52] **There is no immediate need to worry if your tap water is disinfected with chlorine, as this is the case in many places around the world, but still, we recommend buying bottled water just to be sure**.

2.4 Alcohol

With regard to bladder cancer, it is probably safe to drink alcohol.[55] In 2012, a research study including over 10,000 bladder cancer cases provided definite evidence on the absence of any material association between alcohol drinking and bladder cancer risk, even at high levels of consumption.[55] Alcohol consumption may increase the risk of getting other types of cancers such as breast and bowel cancer,[56] so it still not something we would recommend.

2.5 Coffee

Coffee was first considered possibly harmful because of several compounds in it, including caffeine, polycyclic aromatic hydrocarbons, and nitrosamines.[57] Results for epidemiological studies on the relation between coffee drinking and bladder cancer risk, however, are inconclusive. Whereas some studies, indeed, show a harmful effect,[30,58−61] others lack to show an association and argue that the observed harmful effect of coffee on bladder cancer risk is caused by a masked effect of smoking, as we now know that smokers drink more coffee.[45,62−64] Since, however, the largest study ever conducted (and most recent) on the influence of coffee drinking and bladder cancer risk shows a harmful effect of drinking more than four cups of coffee per day among nonsmokers, we should **be careful drinking too much coffee** in our fight against bladder cancer.

Iced tea (drinks)

A few cups of tea a day can make a positive contribution to sufficient fluid intake. For variety's sake, drink a glass of iced tea occasionally. It is very easy to make iced tea and it tastes better than store-bought. You can use your favorite variety of tea and avoid unwanted additives like sugar. Iced tea can be prepared hot or cold.

Continued

Iced tea (drinks)—cont'd

Iced tea recipe
Hot preparation
The easiest preparation is to make tea as you usually do, using the tea variety you like best. All tea varieties are suitable. Make sure to use the right temperature for the variety of tea. With green and herbal teas, it is important to let the boiled water cool first because the leaves will burn and taste bitter if boiling water is used. If you use tea bags, use two bags per 4 cups of water or 1/4 oz. of loose tea or herbs per 4 cups of water.

Ingredients
- 4 cups of boiled water
- Tea of choice (such as Earl Grey, Darjeeling, green tea, green fresh herbal tea, or rooibos)
- Additions:
  - Fresh fruit (strawberry, orange, lemon, grapefruit, lime, peach, mango); and/or
  - Juice of fresh fruit; and/or
  - Fresh leaves of mint, thyme, lemon balm, or rosemary; and/or
  - Fresh ginger; and/or
  - A pinch of cinnamon; and/or
  - One teaspoon of raw honey or elderflower syrup

Hot preparation
Prepare tea and place it in the refrigerator to cool for a few hours. Serve the tea from an attractive glass carafe or teapot and add one or more of the suggested additions and some ice cubes (optional).

Cold preparation
This is just as easy to make, but takes more time and has a stronger taste. You use the same ingredients as for the hot preparation, but you prepare the tea and refrigerate it overnight. The next day, remove the tea bags or loose tea and add the extra ingredients (Fig. 2.3).

Figure 2.3 Iced tea.

2.6 Tea

In contrast to what was thought about drinking coffee, tea has always been considered protective against bladder cancer. The polyphenol compounds in tea in particular protect against damage from oxidative stress and may influence tumor formation and growth and fight against bladder cancer.[65] Two metastudies, combining results from multiple individual research studies, reported that specifically green tea may have a protective effect on bladder cancer,[66] while in Western countries all types of tea may lower the risk of bladder cancer.[67] In addition, a report by the world cancer research fund showed the same for each cup of tea per day for all types of tea.[68] In summary, although there is not yet a great deal of evidence on the role of tea in the risk of bladder cancer, **greater consumption of tea could potentially decrease the risk of bladder cancer.**

2.7 Milk

Milk is an important source of calcium, protein, and vitamins, and it was thought that a higher intake of dietary calcium may have a protective effect against bladder cancer. However, at this point, researchers think there is not enough evidence to make recommendations on the consumption of (cow) milk and bladder cancer.[69] Recently, a study among (approximately),600,000 individuals, including 3500 bladder cancer cases, from all over the world, could not observe a protective (nor a harmful) effect of milk consumption on the risk of developing bladder cancer. Therefore, when forced to a conclusion, we would say milk consumption can be ruled out to have an influential role in the fight against bladder cancer.

2.8 Conclusion

All in all, we are unable to give you an answer to the question, How much should we drink? However, our answer to the question, Does it matter which drinks we choose? would be

Yes! Today's evidence shows that in our fight against bladder cancer, tea is a much better choice than coffee, and whenever drinking water, take bottled water instead of tap water. Alcohol is safe, but we would not recommend that individuals who do not drink alcohol start drinking for any reason.

Carrot and mango smoothie (smoothie)

Introduction
It is important to eat plenty of fruit. Why not make a smoothie? This smoothie combines yellow and orange fruits with vegetables rich in vitamins and minerals. The delicious sweet mango and carrot combine very well with the fresh sweet-and-sour taste of the orange/lemon juice. The smoothie will be slightly spicier with the addition of ginger. I use a blender so I can use as much of the whole fruit as possible, including the dietary fibers.

Smoothie recipe
Carrot–mango–orange and ginger
Ingredients for two glasses (15 oz.)
- 1 winter carrot
- 1 mango or 7 oz. fresh mango pieces
- 7 oz. freshly squeezed orange juice with pulp (or a combination with lemon juice)
- 1 lime
  You also need a food processor, hand blender, or blender.

Preparation
Peel the carrot and cut into $1\frac{1}{2}$ -inch pieces. Peel the mango and cut into small pieces. Squeeze the juice out of the lime. Peel the ginger and grate finely. Combine all fruit with the orange juice in a food processor and blend. If desired, dilute the juice with a little water if it is too thick.

Tips
- Add a spoonful of hemp seeds or other seeds to your smoothie.
- If required for medical reasons, you can easily add a protein-enriched product.
- Add unprocessed breakfast cereals (Fig. 2.4).

Figure 2.4 Carrot and mango smoothie.

CHAPTER 3

Fruits and vegetables in the fight against bladder cancer

Marga van Slooten[1], Maurice Zeegers[2]
[1]Cook & Care, Haarlem, The Netherlands; [2]Care and Public Health Research Institute, Maastricht University, Maastricht, The Netherlands

Contents

Lemon-flavored red lentil soup (soup)

Introduction

This warm lentil soup can easily be called real comfort food. The healthy lentils form a protein-rich basis for the soup. The tomatoes and lemons (both of which contain vitamins and antioxidants) add nice mild sweet-and-sour flavors to the slightly spicy herbs. You can double the recipe and freeze part of it.

This recipe originates from the recipe "Four Corner's Lentil Soup" from *My New Roots* by Sarah Britton, published by Pan Macmillan.

Recipe
Red lentil soup with lemon
Four servings
Ingredients
- 1 Tbsp vegetable oil
- 2 large onions, finely chopped
- 4 cloves of garlic, finely chopped
- 1 Tbsp gingerroot, finely chopped

Continued

Diet and Fighting Bladder Cancer
ISBN 978-0-12-814677-4
https://doi.org/10.1016/B978-0-12-814677-4.00003-4

Lemon-flavored red lentil soup (soup)—cont'd

- Sea salt
- 1 Tbsp cumin powder (taste before adding extra)
- 1/4 tsp cayenne pepper (add more to taste)
- 1 bay leaf
- 14 oz. whole canned tomatoes
- 3 vine-ripened tomatoes
- 2 organic lemons, cut into slices
- 7 oz. of red lentils, rinsed well
- Vegetable stock powder for 4 cups (use the powder sparingly because you can add some to taste later)
- $\frac{1}{2}$ bunch of parsley, finely chopped
- 2 spring onions, cut into rings
- Optional:
    - 1 tsp maple syrup
    - Bread
    - A few sprigs of fresh coriander, chopped

Preparation

Boil 4 cups of water for the vegetable stock and add the stock powder (you can add more later if necessary). Heat the oil in a large pan. Add the onion, garlic, and ginger and sauté for 5 minutes until soft. Add a generous dash of salt, cumin powder, and cayenne pepper. Sauté while stirring for around 2 minutes until fragrant. Add the canned and fresh tomatoes, half the lemon slices, the bay leaf, and the lentils. Next, add the vegetable stock and stir well. Place the lid on the pan and bring to a boil. Reduce heat and let the soup boil for around 30 minutes, until the lentils are done. They should fall apart slightly. If desired, add some maple syrup to bring balance to the flavors. Remove the bay leaf from the soup. Garnish each bowl of soup with finely chopped spring onions or leaf parsley (or coriander) and a lemon slice.

Serve the soup hot with bread (Fig. 3.1).

Figure 3.1 Lemon-flavored red lentil soup.

Brussels sprouts with apple and roasted almonds (main)

Introduction

The following combination of sprouts, carrot, and apple is delicious. Brussels sprouts are included in the cruciferous vegetables and carrots in the yellow and orange vegetables. Almonds contain unsaturated fats, magnesium, proteins, and vitamin E. The apple-pear compote is a delicious side dish or dessert packed with vitamins and minerals. It is very easy to make and you can make multiple servings that last for several days. Make sure to refrigerate.

Recipe
Stir-fried Brussels sprouts with apple and roasted almonds and a carrot and celeriac puree

Fry or cook the Brussels sprouts as briefly as possible or remove the leaves from a number of sprouts to add to the dish raw later to retain all the nutrients. If desired, serve this dish with a chicken fillet and apple-pear compote.

Four servings; 45 minutes
Ingredients
- 23 oz. Brussels sprouts
- 1 celeriac
- 1 large winter carrot
- 2 red onions, finely chopped
- 1 apple
- $1\frac{1}{2}$ tsp nutmeg
- 3 Tbsp almond flakes
- $\frac{1}{2}$ bunch of parsley, finely chopped
- A dash of (plant-based) milk
- 3 tsp mustard
- Salt and pepper
- Extra virgin olive oil

Brussels sprouts with apple and roasted almonds (main)—cont'd

Preparation
Remove the bottom of the Brussels sprouts, cut them in half, and cook them al dente for around 6 minutes.

Peel the apple and cut into pieces. Sprinkle with lemon juice and set aside until ready to use. Roast the almonds in a dry frying pan until they are aromatic and have a nice color. Set aside. Peel the celeriac and cut into 1/2 -inch-thick slices and then cut into cubes. Peel the carrot and cut into slices. Cook the celeriac and carrot with a little bit of salt al dente for 5—7 minutes. Fry the onions in a little bit of oil until soft and translucent. Mash the celeriac and carrot with a dash of milk and add some salt and pepper and a spoonful of mustard to taste. Garnish with parsley. Combine the Brussels sprouts with the apple pieces, nutmeg, and onion mixture and season to taste with salt and pepper. Garnish the puree and vegetables with the roasted almonds.

Optional: Apple-pear compote: Combine 3 finely chopped apples and 2 firm pears with the juice of 1 orange and 1 lemon together with some grated ginger and a cinnamon stick. Cook with the lid on for a few minutes until the fruit becomes soft. Make sure that the fruit does not fall apart. Garnish to taste with dry roasted nuts or seeds.

Tip: Cranberries (fresh or frozen) also combine well with apple. Cook them briefly until they burst open slightly (Fig. 3.2).

Figure 3.2 Brussels sprouts with apple and roasted almonds.

Watermelon with curly kale salad (salad)

Introduction
Try combining fruit and vegetables more often. The combination of curly kale, radish, and cress (raw cruciferous vegetables) with lemon juice and watermelon (fruit) is very healthy.

The combination of sweet, salty, fresh, and slightly spicy flavors makes this salad very diverse and tasty.

Recipe
Watermelon and curly kale salad
Four servings
Ingredients
- 2.6 oz. curly kale salad (or a small bunch of young kale; if the purple version is available, use half green kale and half purple kale)
- 2—3 cups of watermelon, cubed with seeds removed
- 1 small fennel, very thinly sliced
- 1 small cucumber, very thinly sliced
- 4 radishes, cut into thin slices
- 3 spring onions, chopped
- $\frac{1}{2}$ avocado, diced into cubes
- $\frac{1}{2}$ cup crumbled feta cheese
- 4 Tbsp Tahoon cress or garden cress
- 1 Tbsp extra virgin olive oil
- 1 Tbsp lemon juice to taste
- 1 Tbsp white wine vinegar
- Sea salt and freshly ground black pepper

Preparation
Remove the coarse stalks from the kale and tear the curly leaves into small pieces. Put them in a large bowl with a dash of olive oil, salt, pepper, lemon, and white wine vinegar. Use your hands to mix the kale leaves until well combined with the oil and herbs. The quantity will shrink slightly. Add sliced fennel, cucumber, radish, spring onions, cress, avocado, and feta. Add watermelon and combine all ingredients. Season to taste with salt, pepper, lemon, and/or olive oil (Fig. 3.3).

Figure 3.3 Watermelon with curly kale salad.

Research into the relationship between fruits and vegetables and bladder cancer has increased rapidly over the last couple of years. Fruits and vegetables are considered healthy, as they are a rich source of vitamins and minerals that contain bioactive compounds including fibers and polyphenols, which may have protective effects against the development of age-related diseases such as cancer. Another reason that fruits and vegetables are so healthy is that they are full of so-called antioxidants that boost your immune system and thereby potentially help you to decrease your risk of cancer.[70–74] Antioxidants are compounds that limit damage caused by free radicals from cigarette smoke, for example.[75] **But will eating lots of fruits and vegetables help you to prevent bladder cancer? The answer is most likely aresounding yes.** This is why you find many recipe suggestions in this chapter. The network of nutrients in fruits and vegetables is complex, and given the complexity of the situation, it is difficult to pinpoint the effect of one specific food group, but still, fruit and vegetable intake is likely to be one of your strongest allies in your fight against bladder cancer. Most likely any preventive effect results from a combination of influences on several pathways involved in the biological pathway toward cancer. In this chapter, we will explain what is known about fruit and vegetable intake and the risk of developing bladder cancer and what you can do to decrease your chances of getting this disease.

3.1 Fruits and vegetables combined

Because of the biological potential of fruits and vegetables, scientific studies started to investigate whether fruit and vegetable consumption can protect against bladder cancer.[62,76–83] A report on diet and bladder cancer from the World Cancer Research Fund Continuous Update Project suggested that **any consumption of fruits and vegetables combined could significantly decrease the risk of bladder cancer by 3%.**[68] As fruits and vegetables contain different combinations of nutrients, it is likely that individual types of fruits and vegetables have different influences on the risk of bladder cancer.

Velouté chickpea soup (soup)

Introduction
A delicious, mild, and easily digestible legume soup with yellow and orange vegetables. Other ingredients can easily be added to suit your own taste.

Recipe
Chickpea soup
Four servings; 35 minutes
Ingredients

- 12 oz. cooked chickpeas
- 1 medium-sized orange and 1 medium-sized yellow carrot, peeled and cut into thin strips
- 2 cups stock
- 1 onion, sliced into thin rings
- 1 bay leaf
- 1 sprig of celery
- $\frac{1}{2}$ bunch of parsley, finely chopped
- Olive oil
- Salt and pepper

Preparation
In a large pan with a solid base, sauté the sliced onion rings in olive oil over medium heat until soft and translucent. Add the carrot strips and sauté for a few minutes. Add the stock, bay leaf, and celery sprig and cook for 5–10 minutes until all ingredients are thoroughly cooked. Add the chickpeas at the last minute, so that they heat up with the liquid. Remove the bay leaf from the soup. Mash the soup with a hand blender and season to taste with salt and pepper. Serve with the parsley.

Tips

- Add a finely chopped leek, handful of fresh spinach, potato, or fresh tomatoes to the soup.
- Add some lemon juice.
- Add seasonings such as cumin, paprika, or chili powder.
- Add some cress and seeds when serving (Fig. 3.4).

Figure 3.4 Velouté chickpea soup.

Oven-roasted salmon in a parsnip puree (main)

Introduction
This recipe contains a nice combination of vegetables (including orange and yellow, cruciferous, and cress), legumes, and an oil-rich fish. It fits in perfectly with a Mediterranean diet. The dish itself is mild, nutritious, easily digestible, and very tasty. Slow-cooking the salmon keeps it tender and soft as butter.

Recipe
Oven-roasted tomatoes and lentils with slow-cooked salmon and puree made of parsnip, arugula, and potato
Four servings; 35 minutes
Ingredients
- 4 salmon slices with the skin still on
- 11 oz. parsnip
- 4 medium-sized potatoes
- 9 oz. brown or green canned or fresh lentils (soaked overnight and cooked)
- 7 oz. small vine-ripened tomatoes (yellow and red)
- 2 cloves of garlic
- 2 spring onions or shallots
- 3.5 oz. arugula
- A few sprigs of fresh dill
- Tahoon cress* or other cruciferous vegetables
- Salt and pepper
- Olive oil

Preparation
Preheat the oven to 400°F. Wash the tomatoes, finely chop the onions and garlic cloves, remove the leaves from four thyme sprigs, and combine with the lentils in a baking dish. Sprinkle with a little bit of salt and pepper and a dash of olive oil. Place the dish in the middle of the oven and cook for 20 minutes. Meanwhile, wash the salmon and dry well using paper towels. Grease a large frying pan with a spoonful of olive oil and place over medium heat. Put the salmon slices with the skin down in the hot frying pan, cover and cook until tender over low heat for around

Oven-roasted salmon in a parsnip puree (main)—cont'd

15 minutes. Make sure the inside of the salmon is still slightly pink. Meanwhile, peel the potatoes and parsnip and cut into small cubes. Cook for 10—12 minutes until done and mash with a splash of olive oil. Add the arugula to the puree and salt and pepper to taste. Keep warm and garnish with Tahoon cress before serving.

Remove the salmon from the heat, finely chop the dill, and sprinkle the fish slices with dill, salt, and ground pepper (Fig. 3.5).

* Tahoon cress is a seedling with a nutty flavor.

Figure 3.5 Oven-roasted salmon in a parsnip puree.

Orange and fennel Salad (salad)

Introduction

This salad is a delightful combination of yellow and orange cruciferous vegetables (tomatoes, watercress, and cress), fruits (citrus and pear), and green herbs.

Tip: An easily digestible white fish and fresh sheep cheese like feta are perfect ingredients for this salad. Serve with bread for a delicious Mediterranean meal on a hot summer day.

Recipe
Fennel, watercress, and orange salad
Four servings
Ingredients

- 1 fennel
- 2 oz. watercress
- A few sprigs of mint
- A few sprigs of parsley
- 1 box of cress (e.g., afilla, which tastes like peas, or borage, which is a cucumber herb cress)
- 12 yellow-orange cherry tomatoes
- 2 oranges
- 1 pear, cut into slices
- 1 Tbsp Dijon mustard
- A dash of balsamic vinegar
- 1 garlic clove, pressed or finely chopped
- A few sprigs of thyme, leaves removed
- A shot of olive oil

Continued

Orange and fennel Salad (salad)—cont'd

Preparation

Preheat the oven to 350°F. Wash the cherry tomatoes and put them in a baking dish. Make a dressing of the thyme leaves, garlic, salt, pepper, dash of olive oil, and dash of balsamic vinegar. Pour over the tomatoes. Cook the dish with tomatoes briefly in the oven for around 5—7 minutes. They should only cook slightly and preferably remain intact. Allow to cool. In the meantime, wash the fennel and cut into very thin rings. Set aside the green fennel leaves for garnishing. Put the fennel in a large bowl. Peel one orange and make sure to remove the white membrane from the flesh. Cut into very thin slices and add them together with the pear segments to the fennel dish. Squeeze the other orange and sprinkle half of the juice in the bowl with fennel, pear, and orange slices. Also add a dash of olive oil. Combine and set aside.

Dressing: Combine the remaining orange juice with mustard, a dash of olive oil, salt, and pepper. Set aside.

Optional: Remove the leaves from the watercress and combine it with the finely chopped parsley and mint. Sprinkle over the fennel and use the cress to garnish (Fig. 3.6).

Figure 3.6 Orange and fennel salad

Cauliflower soup (soup)

Introduction
Cauliflower and broccoli sprouts are both cruciferous vegetables and taste great combined with yellow carrots. This soup is easy to prepare, rich in flavor, warming, and easy to digest. The walnuts and capers give it a nice crunchy bite and slightly acidic touch.

Recipe
Cauliflower soup with walnuts and capers
Four servings; 45 minutes
Ingredients
- 1 cauliflower
- 1 yellow carrot, chopped
- 1 onion, sliced into thin rings
- 3 cups of vegetable broth
- 3 Tbsp mustard
- 1 bay leaf
- A few sprigs of celery
- Fresh walnuts
- 4 tsp capers
- A handful of broccoli sprouts
- Olive oil
- Salt and pepper
- Optional: dash of (unsweetened, plant-based) milk

Preparation
Slice the onion into rings and sauté slowly in a little olive oil until tender. Make 3 cups of vegetable broth from cubes, bring to a boil, add the bay leaf and all but one sprig of celery (set aside one sprig of celery for garnishing). Next, add the onions. Chop the carrot, remove the leaves and cut away the stalk from the cauliflower. Cut the cauliflower into smaller pieces, setting aside a few florets for garnishing. Slowly boil the cauliflower and carrot in the broth until done. Combine the walnuts and 1 Tbsp of mustard and sauté for 3 minutes in a dry frying pan over medium heat until slightly fragrant and crunchy. Set aside. After around 12—15 minutes, remove the bay leaf from the soup before pureeing. Add 2 Tbsp of mustard and salt and pepper to taste. A dash of (plant-based) milk will make the soup milder and creamier.

Serve with the capers, celery, walnuts, and remaining cauliflower florets and broccoli sprouts (Fig. 3.7).

Figure 3.7 Cauliflower soup.

Sweet potato and kale mash with bean burger (main)

Introduction
A variation on traditional Dutch curly kale potato mash. This version uses sweet potatoes (orange vegetables). Curly kale is a cruciferous vegetable. In this recipe, it is used both cooked and raw to make optimal use of its nutritional value. Walnuts and legumes are both good meat substitutes.

Recipe
Put on your clogs for this curly kale potato mash with sweet potato and black bean burger
Four servings; 40 minutes
Ingredients
- 6 sweet potatoes/batatas, peeled and chopped
- 21.2 oz. curly kale, cut
- A dash of (plant-based) milk
- Mustard
- 2 onions, shredded
- 1 clove of garlic, minced
- 1 crisp apple, cut into small cubes
- A handful of Spanish chestnuts
- A dash of olive oil
- Salt and pepper

Preparation
Sauté the onion and garlic in a frying pan with a dash of olive oil until soft and golden brown. In a large pan, boil the sweet potatoes with a pinch of salt and a little water for 1—2 minutes to cook slightly. Add $^3/_4$ of the curly kale and boil for another 5 —7 minutes. Make sure everything remains al dente! Set aside the rest of the curly kale for later use. Drain the vegetables and mash them together with the onion mix and a dash of (plant-based) milk or olive oil. Add the apple cubes and remaining curly kale and season to taste with salt and pepper. Serve with a spoonful of quality mustard and, if desired, a black bean burger. For the burger, see the next recipe.

Sweet potato and kale mash with bean burger (main)—cont'd

Black bean burger

Ingredients

- Black beans, canned or fresh after soaking beans overnight
- $^1/_2$ yellow or red bell pepper, chopped into small pieces
- 1 medium-sized onion, finely chopped
- 1 clove of garlic, finely chopped
- 1–2 eggs, beaten
- 1/2 tsp (smoked) paprika powder
- A large handful of unroasted walnuts or Spanish chestnuts

Preparation

Roast the walnuts or chestnuts in a dry frying pan until lightly fragrant and colored. Put them in a bowl and set aside. In the same frying pan, sauté the onion and garlic in a little olive oil for 2 minutes until golden brown. Chop the walnuts or chestnuts coarsely. Puree the black beans using a hand blender or manually and add the combination of onions and garlic, chopped nuts, eggs, chopped bell pepper, and paprika powder. Season to taste with salt and pepper. Roll into fine balls and fry for 10 minutes in a frying pan with a little olive oil until crispy.

Tips

- Replace the potatoes with parsnip or white beans and puree.
- This vegetarian version combines very well with the bean burger, but you can also serve it with grilled mackerel fillet or crispy tofu cubes (Fig. 3.8).

Figure 3.8 Sweet potato and kale mash with bean burger.

Earthy Beet Salad with Apple, Chard, and Arugula and a Mustard Dressing (salad)

Introduction
Chard is a leafy vegetable that combines well with other vegetables (cruciferous, yellow and orange) such as arugula, cress, and beet. This recipe brings together a beautiful balance of flavors with the sweet but earthy tones of chard and beet, the slightly bitter flavor of arugula, and the sour/salty flavor of the capers, in combination with the other ingredients. Oven-roasted beets add a sweeter and more intense flavor. To save time, you can also buy precooked beets.

Recipe
A refreshing, earthy beet salad with apple, chard, and arugula and a mustard dressing
4 servings; 15 minutes
Ingredients
- A few stalks of chard, finely cut
- 2 yellow and 2 Chioggia beets
- 1.75 oz. arugula
- 1 apple, chopped into cubes
- 4 Tbsp capers
- 2 Tbsp lemon juice
- A few sprigs of thyme
- 3 or 4 Tbsp raw pistachios
- 3 Tbsp mustard
- Olive oil
- Garden cress or other sprouts
- Salt and pepper

Continued

Earthy Beet Salad with Apple, Chard, and Arugula and a Mustard Dressing (salad)—cont'd

Preparation

Preheat the oven to 400°F. Wrap the yellow and Chioggia beets together with a little olive oil and a sprig of thyme individually in aluminum foil to prevent discoloring. Cook in the oven for around 45 minutes. Let the beets cool and then peel and slice them. Roast the pistachios in a dry frying pan until lightly fragrant and colored and then finely chop them. Make a dressing from 3 Tbsp of mustard, 6—8 Tbsp of olive oil, and lemon juice. Add the capers and season to taste with salt and pepper. Garnish the bowls or plates with arugula, apple dices, and chard. Pour some of the dressing over the beets and spread them over the plates. Sprinkle the remainder of the dressing over the dish. Garnish with pistachios, garden cress, and/or sprouts.

Tips

- Add some chickpeas (as hummus, for example), beans, or lentils to create a great lunch salad.
- Add grilled or roasted fish to create a main dish (Fig. 3.9).

Figure 3.9 Red cabbage salad.

3.2 Vegetables

Even though there are no strict recommendations regarding subgroups of fruits and vegetables,[58] the risk of bladder cancer can potentially be reduced by the consumption of **yellow-orange vegetables** (such as peppers and carrots) and **cruciferous vegetables** (like broccoli and cabbage).[75] Moreover, the consumption of raw cruciferous vegetables could possibly be even more beneficial in lowering the risk of bladder cancer compared to cooked cruciferous vegetables. Isothiocyanates, breakdown products from glucosinolates present in cruciferous vegetables, can potentially alter carcinogen metabolism and thereby protect against the development of bladder cancer. However, during cooking some of the glucosinolates will leach into the cooking water.[78] Also **green leafy vegetables** contain high concentrations of carotenoids that could potentially protect against damage to DNA,[79] and a large study indicated that per 0.2 serving increment of daily green leafy vegetable consumption, the risk of bladder cancer decreases by 2%.[80]

3.3 Fruits

Considering subtypes of fruits, **citrus fruits**,[86,87] pome fruits, and tropical fruits have all been suggested to possibly help reduce the risk of bladder cancer. Mainly dietary vitamin C, which is abundant in citrus fruits, has been suggested to be toxic for cancer cells.[88] Moreover, apples contain a wide range of phytochemicals, which have been found to have strong antioxidant properties and the ability to inhibit cancer cell proliferation. Hence, results from an Italian study and a study including data from 10 European countries confirmed that the simple act of eating more **apples and pears** can help in the fight against bladder cancer.[78,89]

3.4 Conclusion

You probably already knew that **eating a lot of fruit and vegetables helps you fight bladder cancer,** but it turns out that some vegetables and fruits may be extra healthy. When it comes to bladder cancer fighting, you can't beat the yellow-orange, cruciferous, and green leafy vegetables nor the citrus fruits. So, before you go to the supermarket, make sure these items are on your grocery list. In addition, you may want to add an apple, because the phrase "an apple a day keeps the doctor away" actually rings fairly true for fighting bladder cancer.

Caldo verde soup (soup)

Introduction
This Portuguese cabbage soup is wonderfully mild and delicious in all its simplicity and consists primarily of simple ingredients like green cabbage and potatoes.

Recipe
Caldo verde cabbage soup
Ingredients
- 14.1 oz. green cabbage, sliced into thin strips
- 1 onion, sliced into thin rings (or chopped)
- 2 cloves of garlic, crushed or minced
- A dash of olive oil
- 4—5 potatoes, peeled and chopped
- 3 cups of vegetable broth (powder or cubes)
- A little bit of lemon juice
- Freshly ground salt and pepper to taste
- 2 spring onions, cut into small rings
- A few sprigs of parsley, leaves shredded

Preparation
Prepare 3 cups of vegetable broth. In a large pan, sauté the onions for 10 minutes, but do not allow to brown. Add the garlic and sauté for another 2 minutes. Add the potatoes and 3/4 of the cabbage and cook briefly. Next, add the broth, bring to a boil, and let the soup boil for 15—20 minutes until the potatoes are tender.

Continued

Caldo verde soup (soup)—cont'd

Puree the soup using a hand blender and bring to a boil again. Add the remaining cabbage and a little lemon juice and let the soup simmer until the strips of cabbage have softened. Season to taste with freshly ground salt and pepper. Garnish with finely chopped parsley leaves and spring onion rings.

Tips
- Instead of green cabbage, you can also use other types of cabbage or green leaf vegetable, such as savoy cabbage or Italian kale.
- Replace the potatoes with batatas.
- During the last few minutes, add a few finely cut tomatoes or carrots.
- Spice it up using (smoked) paprika powder or a pinch of chili pepper (Fig. 3.10).

Figure 3.10 Caldo verde soup.

Courgetti with avocado and walnut pesto (main)

Introduction
Spinach is a leafy vegetable that combines well with other vegetables (cruciferous, yellow and orange) such as tomatoes and cress. In this recipe, classic spaghetti is replaced with zucchini.

Recipe
Green zucchini spaghetti with healthy spinach, velvety avocado, and pungent walnut-basil pesto
4 servings; 40 minutes
This dish can also be combined with fish or poultry, such as slow-cooked salmon, grilled sardines, or chicken fillet.
Ingredients for the spaghetti

- 2 large zucchinis
- 7 oz. fresh spinach, washed
- 12 cherry tomatoes
- 1 organic lemon, zest and juice
- 1 garlic clove, pressed
- 1 avocado, diced
- A handful of cress
- Salt and pepper

Also required: Spiralizer or julienne cutter and a food processor.
Ingredients for the pesto

- 3.5 oz. basil leaves: 3/4 for the pesto, 1/4 for garnishing (alternatives: arugula or curly kale)
- 5 oz. pine nuts: 3/4 for the pesto, 1/4 for garnishing (alternatives: sunflower seeds or walnuts)
- A handful of arugula
- 2 garlic cloves, chopped
- Extra virgin olive oil
- Lemon zest
- Lemon juice to taste
- Salt and pepper

Courgetti with avocado and walnut pesto (main)—cont'd

Preparation
Preheat the oven to approximately 347°F. Put the cherry tomatoes in a small oven tray, sprinkle with a little olive oil, and place in a hot oven for 5—8 minutes until they are slightly soft. Make sure not to let them burst. Once done, set aside for later use. Meanwhile, place the spinach in a large shallow dish and combine with the lemon juice and a little pepper. Set aside in a cool place for later use.

Zucchini spaghetti
Wash the zucchini thoroughly, cut in half if desired and make spaghetti strings using a spiralizer or julienne cutter. Put the zucchini spaghetti in a bowl.

Pesto
Combine the arugula, garlic, basil (save a few leaves for garnishing), dash of olive oil, part of the lemon zest, and juice in a food processor and mix until smooth. Now add the pine nuts, half of the lemon zest, and salt and pepper. Puree and add enough olive oil to create a firm, creamy substance. Taste and, if necessary, add flavor with the remaining lemon zest, juice, and salt and pepper.

Fill a large pan with a small layer of water, add a pinch of salt and bring to a boil. Dip the zucchini spaghetti in the water briefly and strain immediately. Let the spaghetti drain in the strainer. Combine the spaghetti with the pesto and place it on the spinach. Garnish with the tomatoes, sunflower seeds, avocado cubes, cress, and remaining basil leaves.

Tip: You can also stir-fry some or all of the spinach over high heat until less raw.

Making your own pesto is really easy and a lot tastier. Prepare double the amount and use it for other dishes as well, such as fish or a salad. It will keep for a few days if refrigerated in a well-sealed jar (Fig. 3.11).

Figure 3.11 Courgetti with avocado and walnut pesto.

Red Cabbage Salad (Salad)

Introduction

The combination of red cabbage (a cruciferous vegetable) and winter carrot, apple, and other ingredients creates a very healthy, tasty, and vitamin-rich salad that is both appealing and colorful. This basic recipe can be adapted to your own taste by changing, adding, or replacing ingredients. A few tips are provided.

Recipe

Colorful and healthy raw red cabbage salad
4 servings; 20 minutes
Ingredients

- 1/2 small red cabbage, thinly chopped or shredded
- 1 red onion, sliced into thin rings
- 1 large apple, grated
- 1 winter carrot, grated
- 12 walnuts
- A handful of currants or raisins
- 3 Tbsp extra virgin olive oil
- 1—2 Tbsp white balsamic vinegar
- Juice of 1/2 lemon
- 1 Tbsp honey
- Salt and freshly ground pepper

Optional: 1 red pepper, sliced into very thin rings

Preparation

Roast the walnuts in a dry frying pan until fragrant and slightly colored. Once done, set aside for later use. Make a dressing from the olive oil, vinegar, and honey and add salt and some freshly ground pepper to taste. Combine the fruit, vegetables, raisins (or currants), and lemon juice in a large bowl; cover and leave in a cool place for at least 15 minutes so that the flavors absorb fully. Garnish the salad with the walnuts and, if desired, red peppers.

Variations

- Replace the red cabbage with white cabbage.
- Replace the red onion with white onion or 2 shallots.
- Replace the apple with an orange or blood orange.
- Replace the white balsamic vinegar with apple cider or red wine vinegar.
- Replace the walnuts with pecans or hazelnuts (Fig. 3.12).

Figure 3.12 Red cabbage and rocket salad.

Lemon and pear smoothie (smoothie)

Introduction

You can make this delicious, green, and healthy leafy veggie smoothie in the blink of an eye, perfect for starting your day or as a snack.

Recipe

Sprightly spinach and pear smoothie

Ingredients for two glasses (450 mL)

- 3.5 oz. spinach
- 1 or $1\frac{1}{2}$ pear
- $\frac{1}{2}$ lime
- $\frac{1}{2}$ avocado
- 2 sprigs of dill
- A splash of water

Optional: A splash of unsweetened coconut milk.

Also required: A blender or hand blender.

Preparation

Coarsely chop the spinach. Peel the pear and cut into small segments. Cut the avocado in half and cut one half into small pieces. Sprinkle a little lime juice on the other half, leave the seed in, and save for later use. Squeeze the lime and pick the dill leaves from the stems. Puree the spinach, pear, avocado, dill, lemon juice, and a splash of water in a blender or using a hand blender until smooth. You can add a little more water if the juice is too thick. Divide the smoothie between two glasses.

Tips

- Replace the pear with an apple.
- If necessary for medical reasons, you can easily add a protein-enriched product to a smoothie.
- If you want to make a breakfast smoothie, you can add raw breakfast cereals and seeds (Fig. 3.13).

Figure 3.13 Lemon and pear smoothie.

Rice salad with veggies and nuts (main)

Introduction
A delectable dish that can be served either hot or at room temperature. Legumes, grains, and vegetables (cruciferous and yellow ones, among others) combine nicely with fresh herbs, sprouts, and nuts. The fresh dressing made with lemon juice and olive oil is the perfect finishing touch. If you would like to eat a salad with this dish, a good combination would be the refreshing, sweet salad made with beets, apples, and oranges described below.

Recipe
A green and nutritious rice salad with lentils, vegetables and nuts
4 servings; 35 minutes
Ingredients
- 6.5 oz. brown rice or wild rice, although bulgur and buckwheat are also good options
- 6.5 oz. brown or green lentils from a can
- 8 oz. broad beans or a combination with shelled peas (either fresh or frozen)
- 6.5 oz. broccoli, divided into florets
- 1 yellow bell pepper, cut into small strips or pieces
- $\frac{1}{2}$ bunch of parsley, finely chopped
- $\frac{1}{2}$ bunch of mint, finely chopped
- Garden cress or other sprouts
- 2 celery stalks, cut into thin strips
- 4 oz. unroasted nuts (almonds with skin or hazelnuts)
- Juice and zest of 1/2 (organic) lemon, scrubbed
- Extra virgin olive oil
- Salt and pepper

Continued

Rice salad with veggies and nuts (main)—cont'd

Preparation

Boil the rice according to the instructions and leave to cool in a large bowl. Roast the nuts in a dry frying pan until fragrant and brown. Allow to cool and then chop finely. Once done, set aside for later use. Fill a pan with water and a pinch of salt and bring to a boil. Boil the broad beans for 3 minutes until al dente. Make sure to save the cooking water when straining the beans. Dip the broccoli florets in the cooking water and then strain them. Add the legumes, parsley, mint, chopped nuts, bell pepper, celery, and lemon zest and juice to the rice. Add salt and pepper to taste. Garnish with garden cress.

Salad suggestions: Two raw beets, sliced wafer-thin; 1 orange, peeled and cut into segments; 1 apple, cut into little pieces; dressing from juice of 1/2 lemon or orange; 1/2 Tbsp elderflower or maple syrup; and a pinch of freshly ground pepper (Fig. 3.14).

Figure 3.14 Rice salad with veggies and nuts.

Green salad (salad)

Introduction
The recommendation to eat plenty of fruit and vegetables is met beautifully in this salad. The combination of raw cruciferous vegetables (spinach, water cress, seeds) and the refreshing, sweet taste of pears combine well with the nuts and seeds to give it an extra crunch.

Recipe
A refreshing and sweet green salad with cucumber, spinach, water cress, pear, and mint
4 servings; 20 minutes
Ingredients
- 1/2 cucumber
- A handful of fresh spinach, rinsed
- 1 bunch of water cress
- 1 firm pear
- 1 sprig of mint
- A large handful of sprouts (e.g., fennel)
- 2 Tbsp lemon juice
- 3 Tbsp extra virgin olive oil
- 2 Tbsp sesame seed
- 2 Tbsp raw cashew nuts or pistachios
- 1 tsp honey
- Salt and pepper

Preparation
Roast the sesame seeds in a dry frying pan over medium heat until fragrant and slightly brown. Do the same with the nuts. Set both aside for later use. Rinse the cucumber and cut into thin slices. Peel the pear and cut into small cubes. Chop the larger mint leaves into smaller pieces. Remove any stalks from the water cress that are too hard. Make the dressing by combining the lemon juice, olive oil, and honey. Add salt and pepper to taste. Mix all ingredients together. Top with sprouts, nuts, and sesame seeds and drizzle with dressing (Fig. 3.15).

Figure 3.15 Green salad.

CHAPTER 4

Healthy diets in the fight against bladder cancer

Anke Wesselius[1], Marga van Slooten[2], Maurice Zeegers[3]
[1]NUTRIM School for Nutrition and Translational Research in Metabolism, Maastricht University, Maastricht, The Netherlands; [2]Cook & Care, Haarlem, The Netherlands; [3]Care and Public Health Research Institute, Maastricht University, Maastricht, The Netherlands

Contents

The link between cancer and diet still seems as mysterious as the disease itself. Although, as you have read in Chapter 3, research has provided some evidence that certain specific food items may help to prevent bladder cancer, it has not yet resulted in a decreasing number of bladder cancer patients. Apparently, our current malnutrition is not captured by single food items or nutrient investigations. In practice, our daily intake of food is much more complex. Foods and beverages, as well as the nutrients and dietary constituents they contain, are consumed together, never in isolation of one another. And moreover, most of the food and beverage items we consume correlate with each other and are likely to interact or have a synergistic effect, such that the totality of diet may have cumulative effects. To account for this, researchers are now taking a more holistic dietary approach rather than looking at individual foods or nutrients when assessing diet and cancer risk. However, although this approach has received much attention over the

Diet and Fighting Bladder Cancer
ISBN 978-0-12-814677-4
https://doi.org/10.1016/B978-0-12-814677-4.00004-6

past few years, evidence in terms of bladder cancer prevention is still scarce, and no single dietary pattern has yet been established as a major deleterious or aiding dietary pattern. That said, recent research identified several dietary patterns that at least have the potential to influence our risk of bladder cancer. In this chapter we will provide you with all current evidence available on dietary patterns and the fight against bladder cancer, of which the most promising seems to be the Mediterranean diet.

4.1 Healthy dietary patterns: the Mediterranean diet

The Mediterranean diet is a diet that reflects a way of eating that is traditional in the countries bordering the European Mediterranean Sea, including France, Greece, Italy, and Spain. Since it includes different regions and countries, it has a range of definitions. However, all definitions of the Mediterranean diet emphasize a high intake of vegetables, fruits, legumes, nuts, beans, cereals, grains, fish, and unsaturated fats such as olive oil, and it usually includes a low intake of meat and dairy foods. In addition, it typically includes a moderate amount of wine.

The Mediterranean diet is known as probably the healthiest diet in the world. This diet is suggested to be an effective diet for preventing noncommunicable diseases and reducing overall mortality and the occurrence of several cancers. The health benefits of the Mediterranean diet were first discovered by an American researcher named Ancel Keys. While spending some time in Naples, Italy, he noticed in regions bordering the Mediterranean Sea, people were much healthier, heart diseases were less common, and people had longer life expectancy than citizens of New York, when compared to their own relatives who emigrated to the United States in earlier decades.[90] This led to the famous Seven Country Study, in which Keys tried to explain this phenomenon by focusing on foods that made up the diet of these populations. From this study, it clearly emerged that the diet in the Mediterranean areas, which is low in saturated fat and cholesterol, presented a low rate of deaths from cardiovascular diseases and low rates of cancer. Therefore, from this point forward, the Mediterranean diet has been regarded a healthy dietary choice.

Although research on the potential beneficial effect of the Mediterranean diet on cancer development emerged after Keys's discovery, so far only a few studies focused on its relationship with the risk of bladder cancer. The first concrete evidence of the potential health benefits of the Mediterranean diet in terms of reducing the risk of bladder cancer came in 2014. In this year, a research study[91] conducted in several European countries showed that following a Mediterranean diet could lower your bladder cancer risk by almost 20%. A similar protective effect was later confirmed in an Australian research study[92] among 17,045 men and 24,469 women, aged 27–76 years, from the metropolitan area of Melbourne, Australia. However, this effect was established for invasive tumors only and not for superficial tumors (the most common bladder cancer type; also see Chapter 1). More recently, a research study that combined data from 14 individual research studies, originating from 12 different countries, again confirmed the beneficial effect of the Mediterranean diet on the risk of developing bladder cancer.[93] This beneficial effect was strongest in women. Fig. 4.1 shows the decrease in bladder cancer risk observed by the three different research studies. This figure, in which risks are presented with low adherence to the Mediterranean diet groups as reference groups, clearly shows that the **Mediterranean diet is a good choice** in our fight against bladder cancer.

4.2 Healthy dietary patterns: the prudent diet

The prudent diet was developed to provide a way of eating that is consistent with the American dietary pattern while avoiding an excess of empty calories, saturated fat, and food cholesterol. It provides a favorable balance of nutrients, limits total fat content, and facilitates a more desirable ratio of polyunsaturated to saturated fats. It was first described by the so-called Anti-

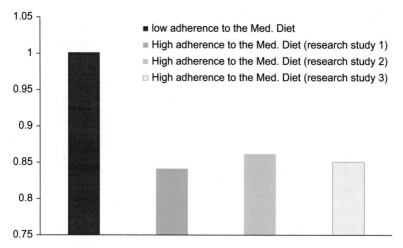

Figure 4.1 Risk of developing bladder cancer according to different research studies.

Coronary Club, a diet and coronary heart disease study project established by the New York City Department of Health, Bureau of Nutrition in June 1957, who had the goal of developing an acceptable experimental diet capable of reducing serum cholesterol in ambulatory middle-aged men.[94] The prudent diet consists of fruits, vegetables, whole grains, legumes, nuts, fish, and low-fat dairy products rather than refined or processed foods, red meats, high concentrated sugars, eggs, and butter. It seems quite similar to the Mediterranean diet, though it features less olive oil.

The Anti-Coronary Club indicated that the prudent diet could lower the number of patients with a new coronary event (i.e., myocardial infarction, ischemic heart failure, unstable angina, or sudden death).[94] This positive effect of the prudent diet on the prevention of coronary events was confirmed in many studies from thereafter, and a recent summary estimate showed that following a prudent diet could lower the risk of developing a coronary event by 20%.[95] Ever since, the prudent diet, like the Mediterranean diet, has been linked to a number of health benefits, with regard to several types of cancer.

The prudent diet as a whole has only been investigated once in relation to the risk of bladder cancer. In a research study conducted in Montevideo, Uruguay, between 1997 and 2004, involving 255 newly diagnosed bladder cancer cases, it was shown that following a prudent diet could not reduce or increase your risk of developing bladder cancer.[96] The researchers suggested that this so-called null finding was possibly the result of the opposite effects of citrus fruits, protecting you from developing bladder cancer, and cooked vegetables, increasing your risk of developing bladder cancer, included in this diet.

Polenta with veggie stew (main)

Introduction
Polenta is made with cornmeal and has a neutral taste. Adding Parmesan cheese or other ingredients like finely cut vegetables, dried mushrooms, or herbs gives the polenta a richer taste. In this recipe, the polenta is baked or grilled and eaten with stewed vegetables. Mediterranean ingredients like eggplants, tomatoes, carrots, olive oil, thyme, and oregano are used. You can enjoy any leftover polenta for lunch the next day.

Add a refreshing sweet salad with citrus fruits, apples, nuts, sprouts, and a nice dressing to complete your meal. See the tip at the bottom of the recipe.

Recipe
Oven-baked polenta with stewed vegetables
Four servings; 45 minutes preparation time (excluding waiting times)Ingredients for polenta

- 5 oz. polenta
- 2.5 cups vegetable broth (you can also use an organic broth cube)
- Extra virgin olive oil
- 1 bunch of basil, shredded
- Salt and pepper
  Optional: 2 oz. Parmesan cheese
  Equipment: Quiche baking tray and grill pan or oven for baking the polenta.

Continued

Polenta with veggie stew (main)—cont'd

Preparation

Line the baking tray with baking paper and set aside. Bring the broth to a boil and add the polenta while stirring. Slowly cook for 5 minutes over low heat. The polenta should turn into a firm porridge. Stir in 1 Tbsp olive oil and, if desired, add Parmesan cheese. Stir in $^3/_4$ of the basil and season to taste with salt and pepper. Pour the polenta into a baking tray and refrigerate for 30 minutes until hardened and then cut the polenta into at least four pieces. Coat all sides with a little olive oil. Heat the grill pan and grill the pieces for a few minutes until nice and crispy on both sides. You can also bake them in a preheated oven at 430°F until golden brown. Keep the polenta warm until ready to eat.

Ingredients for stewed vegetables

- 2 eggplants, diced
- 4 tomatoes, quartered
- 1 winter carrot, cut into thin slices
- 1 yellow bell pepper, cut into thin strips
- 2 onions, shredded
- 2 cloves of garlic, shredded
- 2 sprigs of thyme or oregano, leaves stripped
- A handful of parsley, finely chopped
- Extra virgin olive oil
- Salt and pepper

Preparation of stewed vegetables

In a large frying pan, sauté the onions in the oil for 2 minutes. Next, add the garlic and, after 1 minute, the carrot, eggplant, bell pepper, tomatoes, and thyme. Sauté for around 15–20 minutes over low heat until all vegetables are tender. Season to taste with salt and pepper and garnish with lots of parsley. Serve the vegetables with polenta.

Salad tip

Combine a handful of alfalfa; 1 red grapefruit, skinned and chopped into pieces; a small handful of dry roasted and chopped hazelnuts; and one firm apple, chopped into small cubes; with a simple dressing made of lemon juice, olive oil, 1 teaspoon of mustard, and salt and pepper (Fig. 4.2).

Figure 4.2 Polenta with veggie stew.

Vegetable Curry with chickpeas (main)

Introduction
In both the curry and matching salad, cruciferous vegetables (cauliflower, radish, spinach, sprouts) are nicely combined with orange and yellow vegetables (carrots, sweet potatoes) and fruits (apples, orange/lemon juice), legumes (chickpeas) and nuts. A highly varied, healthy and tasty dish when supplemented with nuts and eggs, this fits in perfectly with a Mediterranean diet.

Recipe
Vegetable curry with eggs and chickpeas and radish-apple salad
Four servings; 40 minutesIngredients
- 1 cauliflower
- 2 winter carrots
- 2 sweet potatoes
- 2 onions, shredded
- 2 cloves of garlic, pressed
- 1 Tbsp turmeric
- Piece of ginger (approximately 1 inch), grated
- $\frac{1}{2}$ red pepper, finely chopped
- 1 apple
- 3 Tbsp tomato puree
- 0.84 cups vegetable broth
- 21.2 oz. chickpeas (either from a can or fresh and soaked overnight)
- 4 eggs, hard-boiled
- Extra virgin olive oil
- Salt and pepper
- Parsley (or coriander)

Preparation
Peel the carrots and potatoes and chop into small pieces. Divide the cauliflower into small florets. Heat a little olive oil in a pan. Sauté the shredded onions, pressed garlic, red pepper, and grated

Vegetable Curry with chickpeas (main)—cont'd

ginger in the oil for 2 minutes. Add the turmeric, followed by the vegetables. Allow to simmer. In the meantime, prepare the vegetable broth (you can use a broth cube if desired). Stir the tomato puree into the vegetable mix; add the apple (in pieces) and the prepared broth. Put a lid on the pan and leave the curry to simmer for 15 minutes over low heat until the vegetables are al dente. In the meantime, boil the eggs until slightly hard. The chickpeas should be added to the curry at the end and only have to be boiled very briefly. Season to taste with salt and pepper. Chop the parsley into fine pieces.

Serve with hard-boiled eggs and parsley

Radish salad: Serve this dish with a fresh salad made of radishes and apple (or pear) slices, baby spinach (or watercress), a small handful of garden cress or other type of cress, and dressing made of orange or lemon juice and a quality olive oil and salt and pepper. Garnish with roasted almonds or walnuts (Fig. 4.3).

Figure 4.3 Vegetable curry with chickpeas.

Spanakorizo (main)

Introduction
Comfort food from Greece! This easy-to-make dish has delicious, healthy, and nutritious ingredients (such as cruciferous leafy vegetables). Spanakorizo is delicious with a slice of feta and fresh or dried oregano and sprinkled with a dash of olive oil, or served with a soft-boiled or fried egg, white fish, or poultry.

Recipe
Spanakorizo
Four servingsIngredients
- 7 oz. risotto rice
- Olive oil
- 1 onion, peeled and finely chopped
- 4 cloves of garlic, peeled and finely chopped
- 18 oz. spinach leaves, rinsed
- 1 organic lemon, zest and juice
- 1 bunch parsley, finely chopped
- 1 bunch dill, finely chopped
- $\frac{1}{2}$ tsp salt
- $\frac{1}{2}$ tsp black pepper
- 1 tsp oregano
- 1 cup of water or broth (if using broth, leave the salt out)

Preparation
Sauté the onion and garlic in hot olive oil until tender and translucent. Add half of the spinach leaves and stir regularly over high heat for 5 minutes. Next, add the oregano, salt, pepper, and water or broth. Add the rice and place the lid on the pan. Cook the dish over low heat until nearly all the water has evaporated and the rice is soft. Taste the rice occasionally and add the remaining spinach and more water if necessary. Remove from the heat. Add a few spoonfuls of lemon juice and, if desired, some zest to the rice and stir. Finally, add the parsley and dill and stir. Place the lid on the pan again and simmer for 5–10 minutes.

Serve hot
Tip
  - Mix a few tablespoons of tomato cubes or puree into the rice (Fig. 4.4).

Figure 4.4 Spanakorizo.

4.3 Not-so-healthy dietary patterns: the Western diet

The Western pattern diet (abbreviated as WPD), or standard American diet, is a modern dietary pattern that is made up of (processed) food that is loaded with saturated fats and refined sugars and contains little fiber and only a few healthy fats (like omega-3 fatty acids). It is a consequence of the Neolithic revolution and Industrial revolutions, which introduced staple foods and new methods of food processing, including the addition of cereals, refined sugars, and refined vegetable oils. The WPD usually contains a high intake of red meat, processed meat, prepackaged foods, butter, fried foods, high-fat dairy products, eggs, refined grains, potatoes, corn (and high-fructose corn syrup), and high-sugar drinks, accompanied with a low intake of fruits, vegetables, fish, legumes, and whole grains.

The introduction of this diet has been linked to the dramatically increasing incidence of chronic diseases unique to civilized Western culture. Inhabitants of traditional cultures that maintain their time-honored diets tend to be relatively free of these Western diseases, and develop them only after adopting a diet that is more Westernized. In 2005, a very comprehensive review, based on 172 different articles and studies on ancestral diets, the evolution of the Western diet, and Western diseases, which were published between 1967 and 2004, concluded that the modern Western diet is directly linked to diseases of civilization such as obesity, type 2 diabetes, hypertension, coronary heart disease, and high cholesterol, as well as to certain cancers.[97] Ever since, many more researchers have found evidence that confirms the relationship between the WPD and many different diseases.

We are only aware of one study that focused on the relationship between the Western diet and the risk of bladder cancer. This study showed that people who follow the Western diet have a 70% higher risk of developing bladder cancer.[96] **The WPD diet is thus not recommended** in our fight against bladder cancer.

4.4 Not-so-healthy dietary patterns: sweet beverages

The first drinkable man–made glass of carbonated water was invented in the 1760s, when carbonation techniques were developed to reproduce naturally occurring carbonated mineral waters. The earliest inventors, however, did not add sugar to these beverages but, instead used chalk and acid to carbonate water. Although it is not known when exactly the first flavorings and sweeteners were added to carbonated water, it was an Atlanta pharmacist, named J.S. Pemberton, who combined kola, a caffeinated nut from Africa, with coca, a stimulant from South America to create Coca-Cola, which is known as the most significant invention in the history of soft drinks. Not much later, legal rights were purchased for Pemberton's formula and the first mass factory was developed. Thereafter, the soft drink industry expanded rapidly, as did the global consumption of soft drinks. The sweet beverages pattern includes soft drinks as its main component. In addition, it mostly includes cordials, fruit juices and drinks with added sugar, sport drinks, and energy drinks. **All typically sugar–sweetened drinks, high in energy density, offer little to no nutritional value.**

Over the past two decades, obesity has escalated to epidemic proportions globally, especially in the United States. Concomitant with this increase in rates of obesity is the consumption of soft drinks and sweet beverages. It is therefore suggested that drinking sweet beverages promotes weight gain and obesity. Since obesity can lead to serious consequences for diseases such as type 2 diabetes and cardiovascular diseases, sweet beverage consumption has become a major public health interest. Today, multiple research studies showed the direct negative influence of consuming sweet beverages and many different diseases, including diabetes, cardiovascular diseases, and several types of cancer.

There is not a lot of evidence in terms of bladder cancer risk, however. So far, only one study, conducted in Montevideo,

Uruguay, established the relation between high consumption of sweet beverages and the risk of bladder cancer. In this research study, it was found that the bladder cancer risk of individuals consuming high amounts of sweet beverages was three times as high as that of individuals consuming low quantities of sweet beverages.[96]

4.5 The Healthy Eating Index

Dietary indices are dietary patterns that are based on current nutritional intake recommendations and dietary guidelines. The most well-known dietary index is the Healthy Eating Index (HEI), which is based on the U.S dietary guidelines. It provides a picture of foods people eat, the amount of variety in the diet, and compliance with specific dietary guidelines. The HEI was originally developed in 1995 in an attempt to evaluate the extent to which Americans are following their national dietary guidelines. Since then, the HEI has been revised and updated three times. The HEI-2015 is the current version of the HEI in terms of conformance with the key recommendations of the 2015–2020 Dietary Guidelines for Americans. This index has been adapted in some countries according to the local nutritional recommendations and orientation.

The HEI-2015 includes 13 dietary compounds. The overall index has a total possible score ranging from 0 to 100, with 100 representing the healthiest score. Each of the 13 components is assigned a standard for achieving a maximum score. The components are then added together to get the total HEI score: a maximum of 100 points. Some areas of the diet are represented by two components and assigned a maximum of 5 points each. All other components receive a maximum of 10 points. Fig. 4.5 shows the different components included in the HEI-2015 as well the scoring standards.

As mentioned previously, the HEI is based on current nutritional intake recommendations and dietary guidelines. Dietary guidelines are produced by experts who review all the available

Component	Maximum points	Standard for maximum score	Standard for minimum score of zero
Adequacy:			
Total Fruits[2]	5	≥0.8 cup equivalent per 1,000 kcal	No Fruit
Whole Fruits[3]	5	≥0.4 cup equivalent per 1,000 kcal	No Whole Fruit
Total Vegetables[4]	5	≥1.1 cup equivalent per 1,000 kcal	No Vegetables
Greens and Beans[4]	5	≥0.2 cup equivalent per 1,000 kcal	No Dark-Green Vegetables or Legumes
Whole Grains	10	≥1.5 ounce equivalent per 1,000 kcal	No Whole Grains
Dairy[5]	10	≥1.3 cup equivalent per 1,000 kcal	No Dairy
Total Protein Foods[4]	5	≥2.5 ounce equivalent per 1,000 kcal	No Protein Foods
Seafood and Plant Proteins[4,6]	5	≥0.8 ounce equivalent per 1,000 kcal	No Seafood or Plant Proteins
Fatty Acids[7]	10	(PUFAs + MUFAs) / SFAs ≥2.5	(PUFAs + MUFAs)/SFAs ≤1.2
Moderation:			
Refined Grains	10	≤1.8 ounce equivalent per 1,000 kcal	≥4.3 ounce equivalent per 1,000 kcal
Sodium	10	≤1.1 grams per 1,000 kcal	≥2.0 grams per 1,000 kcal
Added Sugars	10	≤6.5% of energy	≥26% of energy
Saturated Fats	10	≤8% of energy	≥16% of energy

[1] Intakes between the minimum and maximum standards are scored proportionately.
[2] Includes 100% fruit juice.
[3] Includes all forms except juice.
[4] Includes legumes (beans and peas).
[5] Includes all milk products, such as fluid milk, yogurt, and cheese, and fortified soy beverages.
[6] Includes seafood; nuts, seeds, soy products (other than beverages), and legumes (beans and peas).
[7] Ratio of poly- and mono-unsaturated fatty acids (PUFAs and MUFAs) to saturated fatty acids (SFAs).

Figure 4.5 HEI-2015 components and scoring standards. *(Source: https://www.cnpp.usda.gov.)*

evidence on a specific dietary item, which often includes hundreds of scientific papers. Following the HEI, therefore, automatically should lead to a reduced risk of disease development and mortality. Indeed, research showed that those with the highest HEI-2015 score reduce risk of mortality with 21% from all-cause, 24% from cardiovascular diseases, and 20% from cancer.[98]

So far, no specific attempt has been made to establish the association between the HEI-2015 and the risk of developing bladder cancer. However, following the 2010 alternate version of the HEI has proven to result in an increased risk of developing superficial urothelial cell carcinoma (the most common type of bladder cancer) by 17%.[92] This finding was very surprising, and the researchers in this study, therefore, considered the possibility that individuals in this cohort who adhered more closely to the HEI may have been more health-conscious and sought more prompt and regular medical checks, leading to increased detection of early disease. We should, however, take care to follow the HEI in our fight against bladder cancer.

4.6 Conclusion

For now, we can say that the Mediterranean diet is the most beneficial diet in our fight against bladder cancer. **So, should we all start following the Mediterranean diet? Our answer is yes!** All recipes for main courses in this book therefore adhere to the guidelines of the Mediterranean diet. You might wonder, though, if the trendier healthy diets, such as the Atkins diet, the zone diet, the ketogenic diet, or the vegetarian diet would also be a good way to protect yourself against bladder cancer. Our answer would be **no, unless proven otherwise**! Research clearly shows that even if the main individual food items of a diet are protective it is the combined pattern that counts. It should be noted here that the Mediterranean diet itself cannot make miracles happen. As mentioned in Chapter 2, smoking habits and physical exercise are also import lifestyle factors that have shown to influence the risk of bladder cancer.

CHAPTER 5

Diet during clinical treatment

Maree Brinkman[1], Marga van Slooten[2], Maurice Zeegers[3]

[1]Department of Clinical Studies and Nutritional Epidemiology, Nutrition Biomed Research Institute, Carlton, Victoria, Australia; [2]Cook & Care, Haarlem, The Netherlands; [3]Care and Public Health Research Institute, Maastricht University, Maastricht, The Netherlands

Contents

Maintaining good nutrition and keeping hydrated are important goals for anyone faced with a bladder cancer diagnosis as they plan to undergo treatment. Both treatment and dietary management can also vary depending on the type and stage of the cancer. Some of the standard treatment practices for noninvasive cancer can include surgical (transurethral) resection of the bladder tumor, radiotherapy, chemotherapy, or immunotherapy as described in Chapter 1. Some of these treatments may also be used to manage invasive bladder cancer. However, treatment may differ in terms of application. For example, in the event of more advanced disease, surgery may require partial or radical cystectomy (part or total removal of the bladder), and radiotherapy could be administered in conjunction with chemotherapy. Irrespective of the treatment type, the common aim across all treatment forms is to maintain nutritional adequacy in terms of the appropriate (for the individual) energy (calorie), macronutrient (protein, carbohydrate,

Diet and Fighting Bladder Cancer
ISBN 978-0-12-814677-4
https://doi.org/10.1016/B978-0-12-814677-4.00005-8

and fat), and micronutrient (minerals and vitamins) intake to ensure the best possible outcome.[99] In this chapter we will provide you with information on how you can use food alongside your treatment in order to fight bladder cancer.

5.1 Nutritional considerations for the different types of bladder cancer treatment

There is increasing evidence that the more nourished you go into treatment the better you will be able to tolerate it, and the better you will be able to complete the full course with fewer side effects. While achieving an ideal body weight is generally recommended for cancer prevention, including bladder cancer, weight loss is generally not suitable for anyone about to have surgery, radiotherapy, chemotherapy, or immunotherapy.[100]

Quite often periods of fasting may be required when you need to have tests done or treatment such as surgery. If your calorie intake is low to begin with, it might be further compromised by extended periods of reduced food intake postsurgery or from the side effects of treatment like chemotherapy. Surgery is also recognized as having a catabolic/hypermetabolic effect on the body, which means it increases your body's need for extra protein and calories.[101] Therefore, keep note of any weight changes or loss of appetite and report this to your medical team so that it can be managed quickly and efficiently to maintain your strength and health. Your medical team will be able to advise you regarding how you can manage any gastrointestinal issues such as constipation, diarrhea, or nausea via prescribed medications so you can improve your overall food intake. Psychological factors can also affect how much you eat and drink. If your food and drink consumption is reduced, your medical team will also be able to recommend appropriate nutritional supplements in the form of specialized meal replacements drinks. Sometimes these supplements can be added to your existing food and fluid intake to help maintain your nutritional status and improve your chances of an earlier recovery with minimal side effects.

5.2 Dietary recommendations for pre-and postsurgery

There has been an increased focus on improving the nutritional status and fitness of patients going into surgery. This is referred to as pre- or perioperative nutrition, and there is growing evidence that the healthier and stronger a patient is when they go into surgery, the less time they will have to stay in hospital and less complications following surgery.[102]

Recent recommendations for perioperative nutrition have been to first **identify people who are malnourished and to work on optimizing their nutritional status prior to surgery**. Some of the screening criteria include people with a body mass index (calculated by dividing your body weight in kilograms by your height in meters squared) less than 18.5 kg/m^2 for those under 65 years of age and less than 20 kg/m^2 for those older than 65; loss of weight of more than 10% of your body weight over the past 6 months, and an oral intake of less than 50% of your usual intake (and requirements) in a week.[103] Screening is then followed up with some specific dietary recommendations such as having **1.2 g protein per kilogram** of your body weight, having a nutritional supplement with special **ingredients that will boost the immune system** (e.g., containing arginine and fish oil), and high protein supplements containing 18 g of protein per dose two to three times a day for at least 7 days.[103] These can include a range of immunonutrition products by Nestlé. When food intake and nutritional status is severely compromised, your medical team may recommend tube feeding to improve your condition.[104]

Carbohydrate–rich nutritional supplements such as preOp by Nutricia, which are used under medical supervision, contain 100 kcal/200 mL and 25 g of carbohydrate per bottle. If your medical team decides on this protocol you will have a loading dose of carbohydrate 4 × 200 mL bottles the evening prior to your surgery, and if appropriate, you will have two more 200 mL bottles up to 2 h before your surgery the following day.

Following bladder surgery, you would usually start with sips of water and progress to more fluids, and then a light diet, gradually returning to normal food intake. Recent recommendations are that high-calorie, high-protein foods should be consumed as soon as possible after surgery, and you would keep up this regimen until you resume your usual full diet.[103] These nutritional supplements are generally available in both milk and fruit juice—based forms and can be catered to personal needs and tastes.

If you had a radical cystectomy (bladder removed), a urostomy will be created for you, which is an artificial opening to your urinary system. This will require maintaining your fluid intake and trying to avoid infection.

Sauerkraut with parsnip puree and slow-cooked salmon (main)

Introduction
The uniquely spicy yet sweet flavor of the parsley-bean puree complements perfectly with the fresh sour flavor of the sauerkraut, enriched with diced apples and currants. A deliciously nutritious (lots of healthy vegetables, fruits, protein, good carbs) yet easily digestible dish in which, among other things, the salmon provides healthy fats.

Recipe
Sauerkraut with haricot beans—parsnip puree and slow-cooked salmon
Four servings; 40 minutes
Ingredients
- 26.5 oz. sauerkraut
- 2 onions, sliced into thin rings
- 1 large parsnip, peeled and chopped into cubes
- 8.8 oz. haricot beans, soaked
- 2 firm sweet and tart apples, chopped into cubes
- Juice of 1 lemon
- $\frac{1}{2}$ Tbsp currants or raisins
- 4 salmon fillets with the skin on

Sauerkraut with parsnip puree and slow-cooked salmon (main)—cont'd

- A few sprigs of dill, chopped
- Extra virgin olive oil
- 2 bay leaves
- 1 clove of garlic, pressed
- 1 tsp mustard
- A little bit of mustard cress
- Salt and pepper, freshly ground

Preparation

Boil $^3/_4$ of the sauerkraut together with the bay leaves for 8 —10 minutes in a little water. Set aside the remaining $^1/_4$ to add to the boiled sauerkraut raw later. Heat the olive oil in a frying pan. Fry the onion rings in a little oil until soft and light brown. Drain the sauerkraut and remove the bay leaves. Combine the sauerkraut with the onion rings, apple cubes, and currants or raisins and season to taste with salt and pepper.

Peel the parsnip and chop into cubes. Boil the cubes until you can easily poke them with a fork (this means they are done). Drain and add the haricot beans to warm both ingredients. Mash the beans and parsnip with a hand mixer or masher. Combine with 1 tsp mustard and the garlic. Season to taste with salt and pepper. Garnish the puree with a little mustard cress before serving.

Rinse the salmon with cold water and dry with paper towels. Drizzle a little lemon juice on the fish. Place the salmon fillets in a pan with the skin facing down and cook on a *low* setting with the lid on. The salmon is ready when it is slightly pink (if you cook the salmon too long, it will become too dry). Season with salt and freshly ground pepper. Before serving, garnish the salmon with dill.

Tips

- Add a small handful of roasted walnuts to the sauerkraut and $^1/_2$ Tbsp of walnut oil or add some lightly roasted cumin seeds.
- Replace the parsnip with celeriac.
- Replace the apple with a pear.
- Replace the salmon with chicken fillet or fresh mackerel (Fig. 5.1).

Figure 5.1 Sauerkraut with parsnip puree and slow-cooked salmon.

Chickpea hummus with salmon and stir-fried spinach (main)

Introduction
High-protein legumes (hummus) combine well with green leafy vegetables and delicious fresh fish. A delicious, nutritious, and easily digestible dish.

Recipe
Chickpea hummus with gently cooked fresh fish and fresh stir-fried spinach
Four servings; 35 minutes
Ingredients
- 7 oz. dried chickpeas (fresh or from a can)
- 5.3 oz. tahini
- Juice of 1 lemon
- 3 pressed garlic cloves
- Cooking water from the chickpeas
- Extra virgin olive oil
- 28 oz. spinach, rinsed
- 4 fish fillets with the skin on (e.g., salmon, sardines, tuna, mackerel)
- 1 bunch parsley, finely chopped
- 1 tsp paprika powder (cayenne pepper is also often used, but has a sharper taste)
- 2 Tbsp sesame seeds (or sunflower seeds)
  Optional: Replace the parsley with coriander or mint.

Preparation of hummus
Hummus tastes best using dried chickpeas. Soak the chickpeas overnight in a large bowl with plenty of water. The next day, drain the chickpeas and rinse them thoroughly. Put the chickpeas in a pan with plenty of water and bring to a boil. Skim the skin a few times during boiling and remove the foam with a skimmer. Boil the chickpeas for approximately 20–40 minutes until soft.

Drain the chickpeas, but save some of the cooking water. If you used chickpeas from a can or jar, save the liquid. Put the chickpeas in a blender and mash them until a firm paste forms.

Continued

Chickpea hummus with salmon and stir-fried spinach (main)—cont'd

While blending, add the garlic, tahini, 3 Tbsp lemon juice, and 1 tsp salt. Afterward, add the cooking water (approximately 1/3 to 1/2 cups) to give the hummus a nice thickness. Taste and, if necessary, add more water and/or lemon juice for the appropriate smoothness and season with salt and pepper. Put the hummus in a bowl and leave to stand in a warm place for 30 minutes. Before serving, garnish the bowl with $^3/_4$ of the parsley, a dash of olive oil, and the paprika powder.

Preparation of fish and spinach

Rinse the fish fillets thoroughly, dry them with paper towels, and drizzle a little lemon juice on them. Heat a large frying pan with olive oil on medium heat. Place the fish fillets in the pan with the skins facing down, cover the pan, and switch to low heat. Cook the fillets for 15—20 minutes. Make sure that the thickest part of the fillet retains some of its pink color and does not become too dry. An alternative is to coat the fillets with olive oil and lemon juice and grill them (depending on their thickness) for 2—4 minutes in a very hot grill pan. Serve the fish fillets with freshly ground salt and pepper and some parsley.

Heat a dry wok pan and roast the sesame seeds briefly until they start to color and become fragrant. Don't let the sesame seeds turn too dark because they will taste bitter. Put the seeds in a separate bowl and set aside for later use.

Heat the same wok pan with some oil. Stir-fry the spinach very briefly over medium heat. Add a dash of lemon juice to the spinach and season to taste with salt and pepper. Sprinkle with the sesame seeds.

Options

- Salmon, mackerel, tuna, or sardines are all healthy and suitable types of fish for this recipe.
- Try replacing the spinach with Chinese cabbage (Fig. 5.2).

Figure 5.2 Chickpea hummus with salmon and stir-fried spinach.

5.3 Nutritional management of the side effects of radiotherapy

Your body will also require more energy and protein during radiation treatment.[105] Poor appetite and fatigue are some of the side effects of radiation, so aim for small regular meals and snacks spread throughout the day to maintain your body weight and nutritional requirements. **Nourishing drinks such as fruit smoothies can be an easy way of increasing total energy intake. Enriching meals and drinks with protein powders** (both whey and plant protein varieties are available) is also an excellent way of adding important calories and protein if you have difficulty meeting your daily energy and nutritional requirements.

Other side effects of radiotherapy that can impact your nutritional status are bowel issues such as diarrhea and cystitis.[106] It will be important to **promote fluid and electrolyte intake** via sports drinks and broths to manage diarrhea, and **avoid fluids that can cause diarrhea** such as alcohol, caffeine, artificial sweeteners, and large amounts of sugar, which can be found in soft drinks. Keeping up your fluids will also help to minimize the symptoms of cystitis and you may also wish to seek medical support for this.

5.4 Maintaining good nutrition while on chemotherapy

The role of chemotherapy drugs such as Mitomycin is to destroy the cancer cells to stop them from growing and spreading. If you have Mitomycin as intravesical therapy, which means it is administered directly into the bladder, it should cause side effects only locally, such as cystitis.[107] Having systemic anticancer or cytotoxic drugs (into the bloodstream) can sometimes cause unpleasant side effects, that can affect your nutritional status.

These can include mouth ulcers (making it difficult to eat), fatigue, mild nausea and vomiting, loss of appetite, and diarrhea. The medical team can prescribe appropriate medications to help manage nausea, vomiting, and diarrhea, so it is important to tell your oncologist and cancer nurse as soon as possible to prevent reduced food intake, weight loss, and poor nutritional status. They will also be able to suggest some suitable preparations for the care and management of mouth ulcers.

From a dietary perspective you will want to ensure that you have **adequate fluid intake** (2—3 L per day), **keep up your protein intake** (animal and plant sources), and **increase your intake of foods rich in iron** to help manage symptoms of fatigue; these can include some lean fresh meat (not processed), eggs, and leafy green vegetables. Sipping fluids and having moist soft foods can help the mouth ulcers while waiting for them to heal. Grazing on small regular meals and snacks throughout the day can help to limit nausea, as will avoiding sweet foods, since savory foods are generally better tolerated in these circumstances. Food temperature can also affect nausea and so you may want to **avoid foods that are served hot**. You may also have to **adjust your intake of fiber** according to your bowel function. If you are experiencing diarrhea, reduce your intake of insoluble fiber such as nuts, seeds, vegetable and fruit skins, and opt for more soluble fiber such as vegetable gums, oats, banana, stewed apple, and psyllium husks. You may also want to gradually increase your fiber (insoluble and soluble) along with fluid if constipation becomes a problem for you. Small glasses of prune and pear juice can also help to relieve constipation.

Alcohol can also affect your hydration and nutritional status while on chemotherapy, so it would be best to **avoid** or limit this while undergoing chemotherapy. Similarly, **do not take any vitamin, mineral, or herbal supplemen**t without the knowledge and approval of your oncologist and medical team while undergoing chemotherapy or any other treatment for bladder cancer.[108]

Oven pan dish with endive, yellow beets and sweet potatoes (main)

Introduction
A mild and healthy oven dish in which the eggs are cooked in a hole formed by leafy vegetables, yellow and orange vegetables, and quinoa. Compote is a delicious addition to this dish.

Recipe
Oven dish with endive, sweet potato, yellow beetroot, and boiled egg
Four servings; 30 minutes
Ingredients
- 8.8 oz. endive, rinsed, and finely chopped
- 2 sweet potatoes, peeled and cut into slices
- 2 yellow beetroots, peeled and cut into small cubes
- 3.5 oz. quinoa
- 1 red onion, sliced into thin half rings
- Salt and pepper
- 4 eggs
- $\frac{1}{2}$ bunch parsley, finely chopped
- 2 tsp thyme leaves, fresh or dried

Optional
- A handful of roasted raw nuts (walnuts, cashew nuts, hazel nuts, pistachios) and/or seeds or pits
- A handful of sprouts
  An oven tray is also needed.

Preparation
Preheat the oven to 400°F. Boil the beetroot cubes until al dente and drain. Cook the quinoa according to the package instructions. Boil the sweet potato slices in lightly salted water for 3—5 minutes until al dente and drain. Carefully combine all vegetables with the quinoa in a large bowl and season to taste with salt and pepper. Put everything in a greased oven tray and drizzle a little olive oil on top. Create four holes in different places on the tray and break an egg in each hole. Put the oven tray with the vegetables and eggs in the oven for 12—15 minutes.

Oven pan dish with endive, yellow beets and sweet potatoes (main)—cont'd

Garnish the dish with parsley and, if desired, with nuts and sprouts.

Tips

- Serve lukewarm apple compote with this dish. If desired, add some oat flakes when cooking or add a finely chopped banana after cooking.
- Replace the eggs with fish (Fig. 5.3).

Spinach and sweet potato meal salad with chickpeas (main)

Introduction

An easy-to-make, mild, easily digestible, and varied mixed salad. You can use the ingredients in this recipe to vary the salad to your personal taste. There are a number of suggestions included.

Recipe

Spinach salad with sweet potato and chickpeas
Four servings; 20 minutes
Ingredients for spinach salad

- 2—3 medium-sized batatas/sweet potatoes
- 5.3 oz. spinach
- 2 red onions
- 1 firm sweet and sour apple, cut into small cubes
- 2 tsp mustard seeds
- 1 lemon, pressed
- 8 tsp chickpeas
- 2—3 Tbsp (soy) yogurt
- 2 Tbsp mayonnaise
- 1 small spoon of mustard
- 1 tray of cress
- 1 Tbsp capers
- 2 Tbsp dry-fried cashew nuts, chopped
- 1 Tbsp sesame seeds or hemp seeds

Continued

Figure 5.3 Oven pan dish with endive, yellow beets, and sweet potatoes.

Spinach and sweet potato meal salad with chickpeas (main)—cont'd

Preparation

Peel the sweet potatoes and cut them into 3/4-inch slices. Boil the batata slices in lightly salted water for 3—5 minutes until al dente. Drain and place them on a tray to cool. Roast the mustard seeds in a dry frying pan until slightly fragrant. Make a dressing with the yogurt, mayonnaise, mustard, and mustard seeds. Dilute the dressing with $\frac{1}{2}$ Tbsp water and some lemon juice. Add freshly ground salt and pepper to taste. Cut the onions into very thin rings. Combine the spinach, onion rings, apple cubes, and chickpeas and stir everything gently through the sweet potato slices. Pour the dressing on top and garnish with the cashew nuts, capers, cress, and sesame/hemp seeds.

Tips

- Add a boiled egg, slice of baked tofu, or piece of feta with pumpkin pits and some quality olive oil or a grilled fish to this salad to create a main dish.
- Replace the spinach with Chinese cabbage.
- Replace the chickpeas with a different legume, such as black beans.
- Replace the sweet potatoes with artichokes (Fig. 5.4).

5.5 Immunotherapy with Bacillus Calmette-Guerin

Bacillus Calmette-Guerin (BCG) is a form of immunotherapy using a live attenuated strain of bacteria (Mycobacterium) for the treatment of bladder cancer. BCG is administered directly into your bladder via a catheter, also known as intravesical therapy. You may experience flu-like symptoms such as fever, pain, and fatigue along with other side effects that can affect your nutritional status (e.g., low cell counts including low hemoglobin, nausea, vomiting, and bowel changes).

It is important to keep up your fluid and protein intake while undergoing immunotherapy. Given that you will be

Figure 5.4 Spinach and sweet potato meal salad with chickpeas.

immunocompromised you will also need to **maintain good food hygiene** by ensuring the right food temperature, washing your fruits and vegetables if eaten raw, and avoiding raw fish, undercooked meats and chicken, as well as soft cheeses and pâté from the delicatessen sections of food stores. Ensure that you have **adequate intake of foods rich in iron**. Adding some **foods rich in vitamin C** such as tomato or lemon to (washed) spinach or leafy greens will help aid the absorption of the plant sources of iron (nonheme iron).

As mentioned in earlier sections you will need to manage bowel changes and **note what foods may affect your bowel function** (e.g., foods that are spicy, high in sugars, fats, acidic, or contain large amounts of lactose). It will be important to ensure adequate rehydration if you experience significant diarrhea by having fluids with electrolytes; ask your medical providers what products they recommend for rehydration following diarrhea.

5.6 Should I try complementary or alternative therapies while undergoing treatment for bladder cancer?

If it is strong enough to have an effect, it is strong enough to have an adverse effect, and possibly even interfere with your treatment. After going through often quite challenging treatment procedures you want to avoid either having the effectiveness of your treatment diminished, or the toxicity and side effects of your treatment increased by the interaction of complementary or alternative therapies. Although natural products are seemingly harmless, many of them can have anticoagulant properties (e.g., curcumin). Therefore, it may be best not to do this while you are undergoing active treatment.

Avoid any dietary plans recommending exclusion of entire food groups and beware of claims of curing cancer. Avoid herbal supplements whose ingredients have not been measured (and listed), tested via rigorous clinical trials, and most importantly regulated.

Confer with your medical team about what is suitable and what is not safe while undergoing your care pathway. For more information on herbs and natural therapies have a look at the Memorial Sloan Kettering Cancer Center website's Search About Herbs section.

5.7 Going forward after treatment and long-term survivorship

After completing treatment, you will no doubt have plans for **regular medical monitoring** as determined by your medical team. What better way to move forward toward good health and long-term survivorship than to take control of your diet and make healthy and sustainable lifestyle changes.

As we have seen in Chapter 2, fluid intake is still quite a controversial field when it comes to the risk of bladder cancer. A recent English cohort study of 716 patients with non-muscle-invasive bladder cancer found no association between total fluid consumption and cancer risk, including for alcohol and individual beverages.[109]

As we have seen in Chapter 3, fruits and vegetables contain antioxidants and many other anticarcinogenic properties and seem to be obvious choices for protection against developing cancer. However, the relationship between fruit and vegetable consumption and bladder cancer survival is still too limited to draw conclusions.[110] New research will undoubtedly give the answer to this important question in the next 5 years. For now, we would follow the **same recommendations as outlined in Chapters 3 and 4**.

Stir-fried spinach with tomatoes, white beans and thyme (main)

Introduction

Spinach and tomatoes are a great-tasting combination. The intake of iron from the spinach is also improved by the tomatoes and lemon, both rich in vitamin C. There are tips at the end of this recipe, so you can change some of the ingredients or easily make a few extra dishes.

Stir-fried spinach with tomatoes, white beans and thyme (main)—cont'd

Recipe
Stir-fried spinach or other leafy vegetable with tomatoes and haricot beans with thyme
Ingredients
- 35 oz. spinach
- 9 oz. vine-ripened tomatoes (different colors if possible), halved
- 2 shallots, finely chopped
- 1 jar of haricot beans or chickpeas
- A few sprigs of basil, shredded
- A few sprigs of thyme, leaves stripped
- Juice of 1 lemon
- 3 Tbsp sunflower seeds or sesame seeds
- Olive oil
- Salt and pepper

Spinach
Heat 1 Tbsp olive oil in a large pan or wok pan and fry the finely chopped shallot until translucent. Add the spinach gradually and let it shrink. Once you have added the last bit of the spinach to the pan, add the cherry tomatoes and lemon juice and fry for one more minute. Next, turn off the heat and season with salt and a pinch of pepper. Sprinkle the seeds/pits and basil leaves on top.

Haricot beans with thyme
Drain the haricot beans with a strainer and heat them slightly in a bit of olive oil together with the thyme leaves. Season to taste with salt and pepper.
Tips
- Other leafy vegetables that are rich in iron can also be used in this dish: turnip greens, spinach beet, Chinese cabbage.
- An omelet, fried fish, or chicken/poultry go well with this dish.
- The above ingredients can be used together with a few eggs to make a vegetable omelet.
- Replace the haricot beans with black beans, green lentils, or brown lentils.
- Replace the basil with dill (Fig. 5.5).

Continued

Stir-fried spinach with tomatoes, white beans and thyme (main)—cont'd

Figure 5.5 Stir-fry spinach with tomatoes, white beans, and thyme.

5.8 Conclusion

Following a bladder cancer diagnosis, it is important to maintain your nutritional and hydration status in order to tolerate any treatment as well as you can and to achieve the best possible outcome. Ensuring that you keep up your calorie and protein intake will aid the recovery process from any surgery, radiation, and or chemotherapy treatment, and will ensure you are in the best possible position for going forward as a cancer survivor. This may mean that you may have to have small meals and snacks spread out across the day. You will also need to include plenty of protein in your diet from both lean animal and plant sources. You may find that you will also have to make some other modifications to your food intake such as watching the temperature and texture of your food and fluids. **Be an early responder**—if you are experiencing poor appetite, nausea, bowel issues, taste changes, or any other symptoms and are unable to maintain your body weight via a healthy well-balanced oral diet, consult your medical team for support. They will be able to prescribe antinausea and antidiarrhea medications and if necessary, recommend appropriate nutritional meal replacement drinks and supplements and other nutritional support for you. It is important to check that you have your medical team's approval before taking any herbal, mineral, or vitamin supplement on your own. Many alternative or complementary therapies can potentially interfere with your treatment, and you would not want to reduce the effectiveness of your treatment or increase any side effects.

Egg, veggies and legumes in a pan with Chinese cabbage (main)

Introduction

A delicious one-pan meal packed with healthy vegetables (sprouts, Chinese cabbage, turnip cabbage, broccoli sprouts, and yellow and orange vegetables like bell peppers and carrots), legumes, fruits, and nuts. You can vary the vegetables and legumes to your own taste. The eggs add a tasty element of surprise, but can be replaced by a spoonful of cottage cheese or feta cheese. Serve with a fresh salad and bread for a delicious and easy-to-make main dish.

Continued

Egg, veggies and legumes in a pan with Chinese cabbage (main)—cont'd

Recipe

Eggs with vegetables and legumes prepared in a pan with chinese cabbage salad
Four servings; 35 minutes
Ingredients

- 4 eggs
- 1 can cubed tomatoes (14 oz.)
- 1 onion, chopped
- 2 cloves of garlic, finely chopped
- 1/2 red pepper, finely chopped
- Handful of cherry tomatoes
- 1 yellow or orange bell pepper, chopped into thin strips and seeds removed
- 1 winter carrot, cut into thin slices
- 3.5 oz. haricot beans, drained
- 3.5 oz. borlotti beans, drained
- 3.5 oz. green beans, cut into 1-inch pieces (can be replaced by spinach)
- 3 tsp oregano
- 1 tray of sprouts
- Handful of parsley, finely chopped
- Salt and pepper
- Olive oil

Preparation

Fry the chopped onion with the garlic in a large wok pan with a little olive oil for 1—2 minutes. Briefly add and fry the pepper slices, green beans, and carrots. Add the tomato cubes. Drain the haricot and borlotti beans, rinse them well, and add to the sauce together with the tomatoes. Season with the oregano and freshly ground pepper and sea salt. Create four holes in the sauce and break an egg in each one. Let the eggs cook slowly for around 6 —8 minutes until set. Top with the parsley and sprouts.

Serve with a Chinese cabbage salad and bread

Ingredients

1/4 Chinese cabbage cut into wafer-thin slices
1 small turnip cabbage, chopped
1 large apple cut into cubes
Handful of mixed broccoli sprouts
Handful of roasted pistachios (or cashew nuts or pine nuts)
Make a dressing from the juice of $\frac{1}{2}$ orange or lemon, 1—2 tsp honey, 1 tsp mustard, 3 Tbsp quality olive oil, and freshly ground salt and pepper (Fig. 5.6).

Egg, veggies and legumes in a pan with Chinese cabbage (main)—cont'd

Figure 5.6 Egg, veggies, and legumes in a pan with Chinese cabbage.

CHAPTER 6

Diet in the palliative phase

Marieke van den Beuken-van Everdingen[1],
Marian de van der Schueren[2], Maurice Zeegers[3]
[1]Centre of Expertise for Palliative Care, Maastricht University Medical Centre (MUMC+), Maastricht, The Netherlands; [2]HAN University of Applied Sciences, Nijmegen, The Netherlands; [3]Care and Public Health Research Institute, Maastricht University, Maastricht, The Netherlands

Contents

If your cancer cannot be treated anymore and there are no further therapeutic options available, you enter what is called the symptom-oriented palliative phase of bladder cancer. The focus of your treatment is now on your quality of life to support both you and your loved ones. In this chapter we will explain some of the symptoms and nutritional issues you may face during this stage of your cancer journey and will try to provide you with some suitable strategies for managing the effects of poor appetite, low food and fluid intake, and dramatic weight loss. This chapter does not include specific recipes, as taste alterations and growing lack of appetite will let you choose food by your own wishes.

6.1 What is palliative care?

According to the World Health Organization, "Palliative care is an approach that improves the quality of life of patients and their families facing the problems associated with life-threatening illness, through the prevention and relief of suffering by means of early identification and impeccable assessment and treatment of pain and other problems, physical, psychosocial and spiritual."[111]

Diet and Fighting Bladder Cancer
ISBN 978-0-12-814677-4
https://doi.org/10.1016/B978-0-12-814677-4.00006-X
103

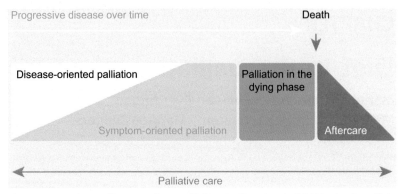

Figure 6.1 The palliative phase. *(Zylicz Z, Teunissen SCCM, de Graeff A, from algemene principes van palliatieve zorg (2010).)*

Palliative care is not the same as end-of-life care. As soon as there are no longer any curable options for a disease your medical team will organize palliative care for you, which comprises four phases (see Fig. 6.1): the disease-oriented palliative phase, the symptom-oriented palliative phase, the dying or end-of-life phase, and the aftercare.

In patients with bladder cancer the early palliative phase will be mainly disease-oriented. Chemotherapy, radiotherapy and immunotherapy may be used to attack the tumor in order to give you the best quality of life and to treat your symptoms, with the aim of prolonging your life. With time and disease progression, possibilities for attacking the disease via active treatment will no longer be possible or appropriate due to poor condition or because the impact of adverse side effects on your quality of life outweighs any potential benefit. The focus will become more on managing your symptoms, comfort, and, ultimately, on the dying phase.

In this chapter we will focus on symptom-oriented palliative care (when antitumor therapy is no longer available or desirable) and on end-of-life care (the dying phase). For information regarding nutrition in the disease-oriented phase of palliative care, please see Chapter 5.

6.2 Managing weight loss (Cachexia)

Cachexia is a word that comprises many objective and subjective findings.[112] Cachexia is a complex syndrome that includes a markedly reduced appetite or total aversion to food (also known as anorexia), inadequate food intake, weight loss consisting of loss of both muscle mass and fat mass, loss of muscle strength, and decreased physical activity. Some of the symptoms you may experience are extreme fatigue, early satiety (or being unable to finish a meal or drink), taste alterations, and psychological distress. In this paragraph we will use the term cachexia as it includes all accompanying features.

As a result of progressive bladder cancer your metabolism will be altered and your protein is used as an energy source instead of a building block, creating what is called a negative protein balance. Your energy stores (muscle mass and fat mass) may become depleted as your calorie intake may become less than your calorie requirements. This is also called a negative energy balance. This can occur due to both your loss of appetite and reduced calorie intake and also from the increased caloric needs from the metabolic changes associated with advanced disease.[113]

As your disease progresses your medical team may discuss the benefit versus the burden of nutritional interventions in your general clinical context, paying special attention to both your life expectancy and quality of life. **Adequate nutrition and dietary advice may gradually be replaced by your wishes concerning the intake of fluids and nutrients** (Fig. 6.2).

This will be especially relevant for more invasive nutritional interventions such as tube feeding (enteral) or total parenteral nutrition. At some point your medical team may even consider stopping tube feeding or parenteral nutrition that was started during treatment if it becomes clear that curation of the disease is no longer possible and the burden of artificial nutrition outweighs the benefits. When we look again at the three phases of palliative care we can summarize:

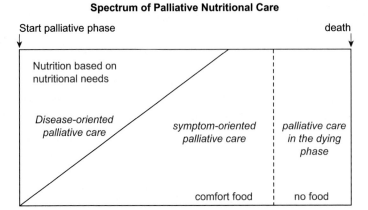

Figure 6.2 Spectrum of nutritional palliative care.[114] *(Bron: LWDO 2013, naar model Spectrum palliatieve zorg, De Graeff et al. 2010.)*

- In the disease-oriented phase of palliative care adequate nutrition is very important as described in the previous chapters.
- In the symptom-orientated phase (with an estimated prognosis of months) nutrition has a role in maintaining quality of life, daily functioning, and alleviating nutritional symptoms. Patients are encouraged to eat enough calories and proteins to keep fit as long as possible, but their preferences in food are leading. As patients approach the terminal phase, appetite will decrease further, patients will eat less and less, and should be offered **comfort food** according to the patients' wishes.

For several symptoms of cachexia palliative supportive measures are available, all aimed to improve your quality of life. If you experience a serious impairment of your quality of life because of anorexia, a trial with corticosteroids can be considered (dexamethasone 4—8 mg, prednisone 30—60 mg). Corticosteroids can improve your appetite and general well-being.

However, the effects are only short-lasting. Megestrol acetate is a medicine that may also improve your appetite in the case of anorexia and is associated with slight weight gain (especially fat mass) in cancer but not with long-term survival.[115] Its use is associated with side effects (i.e., thromboembolism), which should also be carefully monitored. You may want to compare the benefits to the disadvantages that it brings.

Many of the medications used in the palliative phase of your disease may introduce **bowel dysfunction** with multiple symptoms including constipation, anorexia, nausea and vomiting, gastroesophageal reflux, delayed digestion, abdominal pain, flatulence, and bloating. These medications especially include morphine-like painkillers (opioids), certain medications for the treatment of nausea (5HT3-anagonists like ondansetron or granisetron), and preparations with so-called anticholinergic properties (such as medication prescribed for bladder spasm). **Early satiety, nausea, and vomiting** can be treated with prokinetics (medication stimulating bowel movements) such as metoclopramide or domperidon. Adequate laxation is essential to prevent constipation, and pain is treated according to the World Health Organization's three-step pain ladder. All these interventions may contribute to a better appetite. Up to 75% of patients with cancer experience **taste problems**. These vary from altered taste (e.g., metallic taste) or bad taste, to hypo- or ageusia (less taste or no taste at all). Therapy consists of **adequate mouth care**, treatment of oral infections, stimulation of salivation (e.g., with chewing gum), avoiding strong smells, or avoiding metal cutlery. In some patients, zinc sulfate drinks or tablets can (partly) resolve the taste problems.

6.3 Prevent food battles

Food and the act of eating have many nonbiological associations and meanings.[116] This is especially evident in the common everyday experiences of social interaction. Sharing food is a way to express friendship, facilitate social intercourse, or show concern. Not eating is often interpreted as a sign of progression of disease (which is mostly true at the final stage of life), and **forcing or encouraging patients to continue eating may have more negative than positive effects.**

As you become sicker your body may seem to be slowing down. You and your family may notice that you are sleeping more and more, are always tired, have a poor concentration span, are less interested and becoming more withdrawn. This is a normal part of the last months of life, but it may be the start of a battle within families and between loved ones. Try to prevent this from happening. It can be very upsetting for your family or loved ones to see you eat less and less. They may interpret interest in food as interest in life. "Doctor, if he doesn't eat, he will die," is an expression that is often heard. By refusing food, your family may think that you have chosen to shorten your life. The family may feel rejected or unappreciated if they have cooked your favorite meal or bought expensive delicacies.

Therefore, it is important that you and your family, with the support of your medical team, talk about issues around eating and understand that food will not prolong your life. **The last few months of your life should not be filled with battles around food**. Loss of appetite and being unable to eat happens to most cancer patients before death. Food and fluid intake should be voluntary and according to your wishes.

The nutritional impact of symptoms, such as anorexia, nausea, taste and smell alterations, mucositis (inflammation of mucous membranes of your mouth), constipation, dysphagia (swallowing difficulty), abdominal pain, diarrhea, fatigue, inactivity, shortness of breath, or psychosocial distress should be treated and acted upon to improve your quality of life, but if they lead to a diminished intake this should not become a major issue between you and your loved ones.

Not eating may be more comfortable for you and your wishes should be respected when the end of life is near. At this stage, you or your relatives should not worry about weight loss anymore.

Appendix 1: The academic literature used

Maurice Zeegers

Care and Public Health Research Institute, Maastricht University, Maastricht, The Netherlands

1. Antoni S, Ferlay J, Soerjomataram I, Znaor A, Jemal A, Bray F. Bladder cancer incidence and mortality: a global overview and recent trends. *Eur Urol.* 2017;71(1):96−108. https://doi.org/10.1016/j.eururo.2016.06.010.
2. Bryan RT. Update on bladder cancer diagnosis and management: bladder cancer. *Trends Urol Mens Health.* 2013;4(5):7−11. https://doi.org/10.1002/tre.350.
3. Kaufman DS, Shipley WU, Feldman AS. Bladder cancer. *The Lancet.* 2009;374(9685):239−249. https://doi.org/10.1016/S0140-6736(09)60491-8.
4. Babjuk M, Böhle A, Burger M, et al. EAU guidelines on non−muscle-invasive urothelial carcinoma of the bladder: update 2016. *Eur Urol.* 2017;71(3):447−461. https://doi.org/10.1016/j.eururo.2016.05.041.
5. Witjes JA, Compérat E, Cowan NC, et al. EAU guidelines on muscle-invasive and metastatic bladder cancer: summary of the 2013 guidelines. *Eur Urol.* 2014;65(4):778−792. https://doi.org/10.1016/j.eururo.2013.11.046.
6. Wallace DMA, Bryan RT, Dunn JA, Begum G, Bathers S, West Midlands Urological Research Group. Delay and survival in bladder cancer. *BJU Int.* 2002;89(9):868−878. https://doi.org/10.1046/j.1464-410X.2002.02776.x.
7. Knowles MA, Hurst CD. Molecular biology of bladder cancer: new insights into pathogenesis and clinical diversity. *Nat Rev Canc.* 2015;15(1):25−41. https://doi.org/10.1038/nrc3817.
8. James ND, Hussain SA, Hall E, et al. Radiotherapy with or without chemotherapy in muscle-invasive bladder cancer. *N Engl J Med.* 2012;366(16):1477−1488. https://doi.org/10.1056/NEJMoa1106106.
9. Hemelt M, Hu Z, Zhong Z, et al. Fluid intake and the risk of bladder cancer: results from the south and east China case-control study on bladder cancer. *Int J Cancer.* 2010;127(3):638−645. https://doi.org/10.1002/ijc.25084.
10. Bladder Cancer Statistics | Cancer Research UK. https://www.cancerresearchuk.org/health-professional/cancer-statistics/statistics-by-cancer-type/bladder-cancer.
11. D'Costa JJ, Goldsmith JC, Wilson JS, Bryan RT, Ward DG. A systematic review of the diagnostic and prognostic value of urinary protein biomarkers in urothelial bladder cancer. *Bladder Cancer.* 2016;2(3):301−317. https://doi.org/10.3233/BLC-160054.
12. van Osch FH, Jochems SH, van Schooten FJ, Bryan RT, Zeegers MP. Quantified relations between exposure to tobacco smoking and bladder cancer risk: a meta-analysis of 89 observational studies. *Int J Epidemiol.* 2016. https://doi.org/10.1093/ije/dyw044.
13. Reulen RC, Kellen E, Buntinx F, Brinkman M, Zeegers MP. A meta-analysis on the association between bladder cancer and occupation. *Scand J Urol Nephrol Suppl.* 2008;(218):64−78. https://doi.org/10.1080/03008880802325192.
14. van Osch FHM, Vlaanderen J, Jochems SHJ, et al. Modeling the complex exposure history of smoking in predicting bladder cancer: a pooled analysis of 15 case-control studies. *Epidemiology.* 2018. https://doi.org/10.1097/EDE.0000000000000964.
15. van Osch FH, Jochems SH, van Schooten FJ, Bryan RT, Zeegers MP. Significant role of lifetime cigarette smoking in worsening bladder cancer and upper tract urothelial carcinoma prognosis: a meta-analysis. *J Urol.* 2016;195(4P1):872−879. https://doi.org/10.1016/j.juro.2015.10.139.
16. Keimling M, Behrens G, Schmid D, Jochem C, Leitzmann MF. The association between physical activity and bladder cancer: systematic review and meta-analysis. *Br J Canc.* 2014;110(7):1862−1870. https://doi.org/10.1038/bjc.2014.77.

17. Fernández MI, López JF, Vivaldi B, Coz F. Long-term impact of arsenic in drinking water on bladder cancer health care and mortality rates 20 years after end of exposure. *J Urol.* 2012;187(3):856–861. https://doi.org/10.1016/j.juro.2011.10.157.
18. *Six to Eight Glasses of Water 'Still Best'.* NHS.UK; July 13, 2011. https://www.nhs.uk/news/food-and-diet/six-to-eight-glasses-of-water-still-best/.
19. Davis RE, McGregor GR, Enfield KB. Humidity: a review and primer on atmospheric moisture and human health. *Environ Res.* 2016;144:106–116. https://doi.org/10.1016/j.envres.2015.10.014.
20. Braver DJ, Modan M, Chêtrit A, Lusky A, Braf Z. Drinking, micturition habits, and urine concentration as potential risk factors in urinary bladder cancer. *J Natl Cancer Inst.* 1987;78(3):437–440.
21. Mcdonald DF, Lund RR. The role of the urine in vesical neoplasm. I. Experimental confirmation of the urogenous theory of pathogenesis. *J Urol.* 1954;71(5):560–570.
22. Oyasu R, Hopp ML. The etiology of cancer of the bladder. *Surg Gynecol Obstet.* 1974;138(1):97–108.
23. Parkash O, Kiesswetter H. The role of urine in the etiology of cancer of the urinary bladder. *Urol Int.* 1976;31(5):343–348. https://doi.org/10.1159/000280070.
24. Michaud DS, Spiegelman D, Clinton SK, et al. Fluid intake and the risk of bladder cancer in men. *N Engl J Med.* 1999;340(18):1390–1397. https://doi.org/10.1056/NEJM199905063401803.
25. Zhou J, Smith S, Giovannucci E, Michaud DS. Reexamination of total fluid intake and bladder cancer in the health professionals follow-up study cohort. *Am J Epidemiol.* 2012;175(7):696–705. https://doi.org/10.1093/aje/kwr359.
26. Buendia Jimenez I, Richardot P, Picard P, Lepicard EM, De Meo M, Talaska G. Effect of increased water intake on urinary DNA adduct levels and mutagenicity in smokers: a randomized study. *Dis Markers.* doi:10.1155/2015/478150.
27. Ros MM, Bas Bueno-de-Mesquita HB, Büchner FL, et al. Fluid intake and the risk of urothelial cell carcinomas in the european prospective investigation into cancer and nutrition (EPIC). *Int J Cancer.* 2011;128(11):2695–2708. https://doi.org/10.1002/ijc.25592.
28. Zeegers MP, Dorant E, Goldbohm RA, van den Brandt PA. Are coffee, tea, and total fluid consumption associated with bladder cancer risk? Results from The Netherlands cohort study. *Cancer Causes Control.* 2001;12(3):231–238.
29. Zeegers MP, Tan FE, Goldbohm RA, van den Brandt PA. Are coffee and tea consumption associated with urinary tract cancer risk? A systematic review and meta-analysis. *Int J Epidemiol.* 2001;30(2):353–362.
30. Geoffroy-Perez B, Cordier S. Fluid consumption and the risk of bladder cancer: results of a multicenter case-control study. *Int J Cancer.* 2001;93(6):880–887.
31. Michaud DS, Kogevinas M, Cantor KP, et al. Total fluid and water consumption and the joint effect of exposure to disinfection by-products on risk of bladder cancer. *Environ Health Perspect.* 2007;115(11):1569–1572. https://doi.org/10.1289/ehp.10281.
32. Jiang X, Castelao JE, Groshen S, et al. Water intake and bladder cancer risk in Los Angeles County. *Int J Cancer.* 2008;123(7):1649–1656. https://doi.org/10.1002/ijc.23711.
33. Zhang W, Xiang Y, Fang R, Cheng J, Yuan J, Gao Y. Total fluid intake, urination frequency and risk of bladder cancer: a population-based case-control study in urban Shanghai. *Zhonghua Liuxingbingxue ZaZhi.* 2010;31(10):1120–1124.
34. Wang J, Wu X, Kamat A, Barton Grossman H, Dinney CP, Lin J. Fluid intake, genetic variants of UDP-glucuronosyltransferases, and bladder cancer risk. *Br J Canc.* 2013;108(11):2372–2380. https://doi.org/10.1038/bjc.2013.190.

35. Baris D, Waddell R, Beane Freeman LE, et al. Elevated bladder cancer in northern new england: the role of drinking water and arsenic. *J Natl Cancer Inst.* 2016;108(9). https://doi.org/10.1093/jnci/djw099.
36. Di Maso M, Bosetti C, Taborelli M, et al. Dietary water intake and bladder cancer risk: an Italian case—control study. *Cancer Epidemiol.* 2016;45:151—156. https://doi.org/10.1016/j.canep.2016.09.015.
37. Cui J, Bo Q, Zhang N, et al. Fluid intake-to-bed time, nocturia frequency and the risk of urothelial carcinoma of the bladder: a case-control study. *J Cancer.* 2017;8(16):3268—3273. https://doi.org/10.7150/jca.21555.
38. Liu Q, Liao B, Tian Y, et al. Total fluid consumption and risk of bladder cancer: a meta-analysis with updated data. *Oncotarget.* 2017;8(33):55467—55477. https://doi.org/10.18632/oncotarget.18100.
39. Mills PK, Beeson WL, Phillips RL, Fraser GE. Bladder cancer in a low risk population: results from the adventist health study. *Am J Epidemiol.* 1991;133(3):230—239.
40. Bai Y, Yuan H, Li J, Tang Y, Pu C, Han P. Relationship between bladder cancer and total fluid intake: a meta-analysis of epidemiological evidence. *World J Surg Oncol.* 2014;12:223. https://doi.org/10.1186/1477-7819-12-223.
41. Jensen OM, Wahrendorf J, Knudsen JB, Sørensen BL. The Copenhagen case-control study of bladder cancer. II. Effect of coffee and other beverages. *Int J Cancer.* 1986;37(5):651—657.
42. Slattery ML, West DW, Robison LM. Fluid intake and bladder cancer in Utah. *Int J Cancer.* 1988;42(1):17—22.
43. Kunze E, Chang-Claude J, Frentzel-Beyme R. Life style and occupational risk factors for bladder cancer in Germany. A case-control study. *Cancer.* 1992;69(7):1776—1790.
44. Veena JE, Graham S, Freudenheim J, et al. Drinking water, fluid intake, and bladder cancer in western New York. *Arch Environ Health.* 1993;48(3):191—198. https://doi.org/10.1080/00039896.1993.9940820.
45. Bruemmer B, White E, Vaughan TL, Cheney CL. Fluid intake and the incidence of bladder cancer among middle-aged men and women in a three-county area of western Washington. *Nutr Canc.* 1997;29(2):163—168. https://doi.org/10.1080/01635589709514619.
46. Pohlabeln H, Jöckel KH, Bolm-Audorff U. Non-occupational risk factors for cancer of the lower urinary tract in Germany. *Eur J Epidemiol.* 1999;15(5):411—419.
47. Bianchi GD, Cerhan JR, Parker AS, et al. Tea consumption and risk of bladder and kidney cancers in a population-based case-control study. *Am J Epidemiol.* 2000;151(4):377—383.
48. Egan KB. The epidemiology of benign prostatic hyperplasia associated with lower urinary tract symptoms: prevalence and incident rates. *Urol Clin.* 2016;43(3):289—297. https://doi.org/10.1016/j.ucl.2016.04.001.
49. Dai X, Fang X, Ma Y, Xianyu J. Benign prostatic hyperplasia and the risk of prostate cancer and bladder cancer: a meta-analysis of observational studies. *Medicine.* 2016;95(18):e3493. https://doi.org/10.1097/MD.0000000000003493.
50. Claude J, Kunze E, Frentzel-Beyme R, Paczkowski K, Schneider J, Schubert H. Life-style and occupational risk factors in cancer of the lower urinary tract. *Am J Epidemiol.* 1986;124(4):578—589.
51. Saint-Jacques N, Parker L, Brown P, Dummer TJ. Arsenic in drinking water and urinary tract cancers: a systematic review of 30 years of epidemiological evidence. *Environ Health Glob Access Sci Source.* 2014;13:44. https://doi.org/10.1186/1476-069X-13-44.
52. Villanueva CM, Cantor KP, Grimalt JO, et al. Bladder cancer and exposure to water disinfection by-products through ingestion, bathing, showering, and swimming in pools. *Am J Epidemiol.* 2007;165(2):148—156. https://doi.org/10.1093/aje/kwj364.

53. FAO/WHO. *Summary of Evaluations Performed by the Joint FAO/WHO 2006*. 2006.

54. Naujokas MF, Anderson B, Ahsan H, et al. The broad scope of health effects from chronic arsenic exposure: update on a worldwide public health problem. *Environ Health Perspect*. 2013;121(3):295—302. https://doi.org/10.1289/ehp.1205875.

55. Pelucchi C, Galeone C, Tramacere I, et al. Alcohol drinking and bladder cancer risk: a meta-analysis. *Ann Oncol*. 2012;23(6):1586—1593. https://doi.org/10.1093/annonc/mdr460.

56. World Cancer Research Fund, American Institute for Cancer Research. *Food Nutrition Physical Activity and the Prevention of Cancer: A Global Perspective*. 2007. Washington DC.

57. Wu W, Tong Y, Zhao Q, Yu G, Wei X, Lu Q. Coffee consumption and bladder cancer: a meta-analysis of observational studies. *Sci Rep*. 2015;5:9051. https://doi.org/10.1038/srep09051.

58. Vena JE, Freudenheim J, Graham S, et al. Coffee, cigarette smoking, and bladder cancer in Western New York. *Ann Epidemiol*. 1993;3(6):586—591. https://doi.org/10.1016/1047-2797(93)90079-J.

59. De Stefani E, Boffetta P, Deneo-Pellegrini H, et al. Non-alcoholic beverages and risk of bladder cancer in Uruguay. *BMC Canc*. 2007;7:57. https://doi.org/10.1186/1471-2407-7-57.

60. Chyou P-H, Nomura AMY, Stemmermann GN. A prospective study of diet, smoking, and lower urinary tract cancer. *Ann Epidemiol*. 1993;3(3):211—216. https://doi.org/10.1016/1047-2797(93)90021-U.

61. Loftfield E, Freedman ND, Inoue-Choi M, Graubard BI, Sinha R. A prospective investigation of coffee drinking and bladder cancer incidence in the United States. *Epidemiology*. 2017;28(5):685—693. https://doi.org/10.1097/EDE.0000000000000676.

62. Nagano J, Kono S, Preston DL, et al. Bladder-cancer incidence in relation to vegetable and fruit consumption: a prospective study of atomic-bomb survivors. *Int J Cancer*. 2000;86(1):132—138.

63. Demirel F, Cakan M, Yalçinkaya F, Topcuoglu M, Altug U. The association between personal habits and bladder cancer in Turkey. *Int Urol Nephrol*. 2008;40(3):643—647. https://doi.org/10.1007/s11255-008-9331-1.

64. Kobeissi LH, Yassine IA, Jabbour ME, Moussa MA, Dhaini HR. Urinary bladder cancer risk factors: a Lebanese case- control study. *Asian Pac J Cancer Prev APJCP*. 2013;14(5):3205—3211.

65. Yang CS, Wang H, Li GX, Yang Z, Guan F, Jin H. Cancer prevention by tea: evidence from laboratory studies. *Pharmacol Res*. 2011;64(2):113—122. https://doi.org/10.1016/j.phrs.2011.03.001.

66. Wang X, Lin Y-W, Wang S, et al. A meta-analysis of tea consumption and the risk of bladder cancer. *Urol Int*. 2013;90(1):10—16. https://doi.org/10.1159/000342804.

67. Zhang Y-F, Xu Q, Lu J, et al. Tea consumption and the incidence of cancer: a systematic review and meta-analysis of prospective observational studies. *Eur J Cancer Prev*. 2015;24(4):353—362. https://doi.org/10.1097/CEJ.0000000000000094.

68. World Cancer Research Fund International/American Institute for Cancer. Diet, nutrition, physical activity and bladder cancer. In: *Food Nutrition Physical Activity and the Prevention of Cancer: A Global Perspective*. 2018.

69. Li F, An S, Zhou Y, et al. Milk and dairy consumption and risk of bladder cancer: a meta-analysis. *Urology*. 2011;78(6):1298—1305. https://doi.org/10.1016/j.urology.2011.09.002.

70. Hardy TM, Tollefsbol TO. Epigenetic diet: impact on the epigenome and cancer. *Epigenomics*. 2011;3(4):503—518. https://doi.org/10.2217/epi.11.71.

71. Daniel M, Tollefsbol TO. Epigenetic linkage of aging, cancer and nutrition. *J Exp Biol*. 2015;218(1):59—70. https://doi.org/10.1242/jeb.107110.

72. Béliveau R, Gingras D. Role of nutrition in preventing cancer. *Can Fam Physician.* 2007;53(11):1905−1911.
73. Surh Y-J. Cancer chemoprevention with dietary phytochemicals. *Nat Rev Canc.* 2003;3(10):768−780. https://doi.org/10.1038/nrc1189.
74. Veeranki OL, Bhattacharya A, Tang L, Marshall JR, Zhang Y. Cruciferous vegetables, isothiocyanates, and prevention of bladder cancer. *Curr Pharmacol Rep.* 2015;1(4):272−282. https://doi.org/10.1007/s40495-015-0024-z.
75. Kellen E, Zeegers M, Paulussen A, Van Dongen M, Buntinx F. Fruit consumption reduces the effect of smoking on bladder cancer risk. The Belgian case control study on bladder cancer. *Int J Cancer.* 2006;118(10):2572−2578. https://doi.org/10.1002/ijc.21714.
76. Larsson SC, Andersson S-O, Johansson J-E, Wolk A. Fruit and vegetable consumption and risk of bladder cancer: a prospective cohort study. *Cancer Epidemiol Biomark Prev.* 2008;17(9):2519−2522. https://doi.org/10.1158/1055-9965.EPI-08-0407.
77. Michaud DS, Spiegelman D, Clinton SK, Rimm EB, Willett WC, Giovannucci EL. Fruit and vegetable intake and incidence of bladder cancer in a male prospective cohort. *J Natl Cancer Inst.* 1999;91(7):605−613.
78. Büchner FL, Bueno-de-Mesquita HB, Ros MM, et al. Consumption of vegetables and fruit and the risk of bladder cancer in the european prospective investigation into cancer and nutrition. *Int J Cancer.* 2009;125(11):2643−2651. https://doi.org/10.1002/ijc.24582.
79. Zeegers MP, Goldbohm RA, van den Brandt PA. Consumption of vegetables and fruits and urothelial cancer incidence: a prospective study. *Cancer Epidemiol Biomark Prev.* 2001;10(11):1121−1128.
80. Holick CN, De Vivo I, Feskanich D, Giovannucci E, Stampfer M, Michaud DS. Intake of fruits and vegetables, carotenoids, folate, and vitamins A, C, E and risk of bladder cancer among women (United States). *Cancer Causes Control.* 2005;16(10):1135−1145. https://doi.org/10.1007/s10552-005-0337-z.
81. Park S-Y, Ollberding NJ, Woolcott CG, Wilkens LR, Henderson BE, Kolonel LN. Fruit and vegetable intakes are associated with lower risk of bladder cancer among women in the multiethnic cohort study. *J Nutr.* 2013;143(8):1283−1292. https://doi.org/10.3945/jn.113.174920.
82. Fankhauser CD, Mostafid H. Prevention of bladder cancer incidence and recurrence: nutrition and lifestyle. *Curr Opin Urol.* 2018;28(1):88−92. https://doi.org/10.1097/MOU.0000000000000452.
83. Al-Zalabani AH, Stewart KF, Wesselius A, Schols AM, Zeegers MP. Modifiable risk factors for the prevention of bladder cancer: a systematic review of meta-analyses. *Eur J Epidemiol.* 2016;31(9):811−851. https://doi.org/10.1007/s10654-016-0138-6.
84. Tang L, Zirpoli GR, Guru K, et al. Consumption of raw cruciferous vegetables is inversely associated with bladder cancer risk. *Cancer Epidemiol Biomark Prev.* 2008;17(4):938−944. https://doi.org/10.1158/1055-9965.EPI-07-2502.
85. Azqueta A, Collins AR. Carotenoids and DNA damage. *Mutat Res.* 2012;733(1−2):4−13. https://doi.org/10.1016/j.mrfmmm.2012.03.005.
86. Xu C, Zeng X-T, Liu T-Z, et al. Fruits and vegetables intake and risk of bladder cancer: a PRISMA-compliant systematic review and dose-response meta-analysis of prospective cohort studies. *Medicine.* 2015;94(17):e759. https://doi.org/10.1097/MD.0000000000000759.
87. Liang S, Lv G, Chen W, Jiang J, Wang J. Citrus fruit intake and bladder cancer risk: a meta-analysis of observational studies. *Int J Food Sci Nutr.* 2014;65(7):893−898. https://doi.org/10.3109/09637486.2014.917151.
88. Vissers MCM, Das AB. Potential mechanisms of action for vitamin C in cancer: reviewing the evidence. *Front Physiol.* 2018;9. https://doi.org/10.3389/fphys.2018.00809.

89. Sacerdote C, Matullo G, Polidoro S, et al. Intake of fruits and vegetables and polymorphisms in DNA repair genes in bladder cancer. *Mutagenesis.* 2007;22(4):281—285. https://doi.org/10.1093/mutage/gem014.

90. Keys AB, Keys M. *How to Eat Well and Stay Well the Mediterranean Way.* 1st ed. Garden City, N.Y: Doubleday; 1975.

91. Buckland G, Ros MM, Roswall N, et al. Adherence to the Mediterranean diet and risk of bladder cancer in the EPIC cohort study. *Int J Cancer.* 2014;134(10):2504—2511. https://doi.org/10.1002/ijc.28573.

92. Dugué P-A, Hodge AM, Brinkman MT, et al. Association between selected dietary scores and the risk of urothelial cell carcinoma: a prospective cohort study: healthy diet scores and risk of UCC. *Int J Cancer.* 2016;139(6):1251—1260. https://doi.org/10.1002/ijc.30175.

93. Witlox WJA, van Osch FHM, Brinkman M, et al. An inverse association between the Mediterranean diet and bladder cancer risk: a pooled analysis of 13 cohort studies. *Eur J Nutr.* 2019. https://doi.org/10.1007/s00394-019-01907-8.

94. Singman HS, Berman SN, Cowell C, Maslansky E, Archer M. The anti-coronary club: 1957 to 1972. *Am J Clin Nutr.* 1980;33(6):1183—1191. https://doi.org/10.1093/ajcn/33.6.1183.

95. Hou L, Li F, Wang Y, et al. Association between dietary patterns and coronary heart disease: a meta-analysis of prospective cohort studies. *Int J Clin Exp Med.* 2015;8(1):781—790.

96. De Stefani E, Deneo-Pellegrini H, Boffetta P, et al. Dietary patterns and risk of cancer: a factor analysis in Uruguay. *Int J Cancer.* 2009;124(6):1391—1397. https://doi.org/10.1002/ijc.24035.

97. Cordain L, Eaton SB, Sebastian A, et al. Origins and evolution of the western diet: health implications for the 21st century. *Am J Clin Nutr.* 2005;81(2):341—354. https://doi.org/10.1093/ajcn.81.2.341.

98. Panizza C, Shvetsov Y, Harmon B, et al. Testing the predictive validity of the healthy eating index-2015 in the multiethnic cohort: is the score associated with a reduced risk of all-cause and cause-specific mortality? *Nutrients.* 2018;10(4):452. https://doi.org/10.3390/nu10040452.

99. Arora K, Hanson KT, Habermann EB, Tollefson MK, Psutka SP. Early complications and mortality following radical cystectomy: associations with malnutrition and obesity. *Bladder Cancer.* 2018;4(4):377—388. https://doi.org/10.3233/BLC-180173.

100. McDonald ML, Liss MA, Nseyo UU, Gal DB, Kane CJ, Kader AK. Weight loss following radical cystectomy for bladder cancer: characterization and effect on survival. *Clin Genitourin Cancer.* 2017;15(1):86—92. https://doi.org/10.1016/j.clgc.2016.06.009.

101. Tobert CM, Hamilton-Reeves JM, Norian LA, et al. Emerging impact of malnutrition on surgical patients: literature review and potential implications for cystectomy in bladder cancer. *J Urol.* 2017;198(3):511—519. https://doi.org/10.1016/j.juro.2017.01.087.

102. Oberle AD, West JM, Tobert CM, Conley GL, Nepple KG. Optimizing nutrition prior to radical cystectomy. *Curr Urol Rep.* 2018;19(12). https://doi.org/10.1007/s11934-018-0854-4.

103. Wischmeyer PE, Carli F, Evans DC, et al. American society for enhanced recovery and perioperative quality initiative joint consensus statement on nutrition screening and therapy within a surgical enhanced recovery pathway. *Anesth Analg.* 2018;126(6):1883—1895. https://doi.org/10.1213/ANE.0000000000002743.

104. Arends J, Bachmann P, Baracos V, et al. ESPEN guidelines on nutrition in cancer patients. *Clin Nutr.* 2017;36(1):11—48. https://doi.org/10.1016/j.clnu.2016.07.015.

105. Isenring EA, Bauer JD, Capra S. Nutrition support using the American dietetic association medical nutrition therapy protocol for radiation oncology patients improves dietary

intake compared with standard practice. *J Am Diet Assoc.* 2007;107(3):404−412. https://doi.org/10.1016/j.jada.2006.12.007.

106. Mallick S, Madan R, Julka PK, Rath GK. Radiation induced cystitis and proctitis - prediction, assessment and management. *Asian Pac J Cancer Prev.* 2015;16(14):5589−5594.

107. Cancer Research UK. Side Effects of Mitomycin C. https://www.cancerresearchuk.org/about-cancer/cancer-in-general/treatment/cancer-drugs/drugs/mitomycinc/side-effects.

108. Ben-Arye E, Samuels N, Goldstein LH, et al. Potential risks associated with traditional herbal medicine use in cancer care: a study of middle eastern oncology health care professionals: risks associated with herbal use. *Cancer.* 2016;122(4):598−610. https://doi.org/10.1002/cncr.29796.

109. Jochems SHJ, Van Osch FHM, Bryan RT, et al. Impact of dietary patterns and the main food groups on mortality and recurrence in cancer survivors: a systematic review of current epidemiological literature. *BMJ Open.* 2018;8(2):e014530. https://doi.org/10.1136/bmjopen-2016-014530.

110. Jochems SHJ, van Osch FHM, Reulen RC, et al. Fruit and vegetable intake and the risk of recurrence in patients with non-muscle invasive bladder cancer: a prospective cohort study. *Cancer Causes Control.* 2018;29(6):573−579. https://doi.org/10.1007/s10552-018-1029-9.

111. WHO. Definition of Palliative Care. https://www.who.int/cancer/palliative/definition/en/.

112. Fearon K, Strasser F, Anker SD, et al. Definition and classification of cancer cachexia: an international consensus. *Lancet Oncol.* 2011;12(5):489−495. https://doi.org/10.1016/S1470-2045(10)70218-7.

113. Fearon KCH, Glass DJ, Guttridge DC. Cancer cachexia: mediators, signaling, and metabolic pathways. *Cell Metabol.* 2012;16(2):153−166. https://doi.org/10.1016/j.cmet.2012.06.011.

114. Cederholm T, Barazzoni R, Austin P, et al. ESPEN guidelines on definitions and terminology of clinical nutrition. *Clin Nutr.* 2017;36(1):49−64. https://doi.org/10.1016/j.clnu.2016.09.004.

115. Ruiz Garcia V, López-Briz E, Carbonell Sanchis R, Gonzalvez Perales JL, Bort-Marti S. Megestrol acetate for treatment of anorexia-cachexia syndrome. *Cochrane Database Syst Rev.* 2013;3:CD004310. https://doi.org/10.1002/14651858.CD004310.pub3.

116. Fieldhouse P. Social functions of food. In: Fieldhouse P, ed. *Food and Nutrition: Customs and Culture.* Boston, MA: Springer US; 1995:78−105. https://doi.org/10.1007/978-1-4899-3256-3_4.

Appendix 2: How the recipes relate

Marga van Slooten
Cook & Care, Haarlem, The Netherlands

Does the recipe contain:	Cruciferous vegetables	Raw cruciferous vegetables	Leafy vegetables	Yellow orange vegetables in combination with cruciferous vegetables	Combination of fruit and vegetables	Apples and pears or citrus fruit	Legumes or lentils	Fatty fish or lean meat	Dairy	Nuts or seeds	Fit in the Mediterranean diet
Chapter 2: Fluids											
H2						Yes					Yes
Fruity Water						Yes					Yes
H2											
Ice tea					Yes	Yes				Included as a suggestion	Yes
H2 Carrot–mango smoothie											
Chapter 3: Fruits and Vegetables											
Lemon-flavored lentil soup			Yes		Yes	Yes	Yes			Yes	Yes
Brussels sprouts with apple and roasted almonds	Yes	Included as a suggestion	Yes	Yes	Yes	Yes		Included as a suggestion		Yes	Yes
Watermelon with curly kale salad	Yes	Yes	Yes		Yes	Yes			Yes		
Velouté chickpea soup	Yes, included as a suggestion	Yes, included as a suggestion	Yes	Yes, if suggestion is included			Yes			Included as a suggestion	Yes

Oven-roasted salmon in a parsnip puree	Yes	Yes	Yes	Yes			Yes	Yes		Yes
Orange-fennel salad	Yes	Yes	Yes	Yes	Yes	Yes		Included as a suggestion	Included as a suggestion	Yes
Cauliflower soup	Yes	Yes	Yes	Yes			Included as a suggestion	Included as a suggestion		Yes
Sweet potato kale mash with bean burger	Yes	Yes	Yes	Yes	Yes	Yes	Yes	Yes	Yes	Yes
Red cabbage salad	Yes		Yes	Yes	Yes	Yes				Yes
Caldo verde soup	Yes	Yes	Yes	Yes	Yes					Yes
Courgetti with avocado-walnut pesto	Yes	Yes	Yes	Yes	Yes	Yes	Included as a suggestion	Included as a suggestion		Yes
Chioggia beet rocket salad	Yes	Yes	Yes	Yes	Yes	Yes	Included as a suggestion	Included as a suggestion	Yes	Yes
Lemon-pear smoothie		Yes		Yes	Yes	Yes			Included as a suggestion	Yes

Continued

Does the recipe contain:	Cruciferous vegetables	Raw cruciferous vegetables	Leafy vegetables	Yellow orange vegetables in combination with cruciferous vegetables	Combination of fruit and vegetables	Apples and pears or citrus fruit	Legumes or lentils	Fatty fish or lean meat	Dairy	Nuts or seeds	Fit in the Mediterranean diet
Rice salad with veggies and nuts	Yes	Yes	Yes	Yes	Yes, included in the salad suggestion	Yes	Yes			Yes	Yes
Green salad	Yes	Yes	Yes		Yes	Yes				Yes	Yes
Chapter 4: Healthy Diets											
Polenta with veggie stew			Yes	Yes, if salad suggestion is included	Yes, if salad suggestion is included	Yes, if salad suggestion is included			Included as a suggestion	Yes, if salad suggestion is included	Yes
Vegetable curry with chickpeas	Yes	Yes, if salad suggestion is included	Yes, if salad suggestion is included	Yes	Yes, if salad suggestion is included	Yes, if salad suggestion is included	Yes		Yes	Yes	Yes
Spanakorizo			Yes		Yes	Yes		Included as a suggestion	Included as a suggestion		Yes
Chapter 5: Diet during Clinical Treatment											
Sauerkraut with parsnip puree and slow cooked Salmon	Yes	Yes			Yes	Yes	Yes	Yes		Yes	Yes

Chickpea hummus with salmon and stir-fried spinach	Included as a suggestion	Yes			Yes	Yes	Yes	Yes	Yes	Yes
Oven pan dish with endive, yellow beets, and sweet potatoes		Yes	Yes, if apple-compote suggestion is included	Yes, if apple-compote suggestion is included	Yes		Included as a suggestion	Yes	Included as a suggestion	Yes
Spinach—sweet potato meal salad with chickpeas	Yes	Yes	Yes	Yes	Yes	Yes	Included as a suggestion	Included as a suggestion	Yes	Yes
Stir-fry spinach with tomatoes, white beans, and thyme		Yes			Yes	Yes	Included as a suggestion	Included as a suggestion	Yes	Yes
Egg, veggies, and legumes in a pan with Chinese cabbage	Yes	Yes	Yes, if salad suggestion is included	Yes, if salad suggestion is included	Yes	Yes		Yes	Yes	Yes

Index

'*Note:* Page numbers followed by "f" indicate figures, "t" indicate tables and "b" indicate boxes.'

Printed in the United States
By Bookmasters